IT WIL
BE TAKEN AWA
FROM HER

A feminist engagement with women's Christian experience

FRAN PORTER

DARTON · LONGMAN + TODD

WHO'S ASKING?

Preamble

I have become quite suspicious of a question that is sometimes heard in church. It's the 'why do women stay?' question. You hear it as a response when women raise any disquiet over their status or position within Christianity. The question has other forms, such as the argument, 'it's the women who support the status quo'. This is sometimes put more negatively as, 'women are their own worst enemies'. But the core meaning is, 'If women are not happy with the way things are, then why do they stay?'

On the surface this appears to be a valid question, worthy of an answer. Over the years, however, I have come to view it differently. I now see it as a question that is a way of deflecting from the real concerns that created it in the first place, namely, women's struggles with their Christian experience *as women*. Rather than paying attention to what women are saying, it puts the focus back on women, either to justify themselves or take the blame for their situation. It is as clever a tool as ridicule in distracting and undermining any who wish to talk about women's status within Christianity. It's a way of saying, 'If it is a problem at all, then it's your problem not ours.'

I am not suggesting that the 'why do women stay?' question is necessarily used consciously in this manner. Indeed, it is more likely that it flows logically from the stance that does not take seriously women's concerns in the first place. After all, if you do not think that there is any real issue over women's identity and place within Christianity, then why would you stop and reflect on the church and faith as a whole?

This is why I have written this book. It is an attempt to illuminate, illustrate and make visible the diminished status of Christian women in their faith. Women occupy a subordinate position by virtue of the way Christian faith is understood and practised. And yet there is little real understanding of this within the Christian community. Until there is genuine and considerable grappling with this situation we can expect little change in the way things are. For if we do not grasp the nature of the problem, how can we expect to address it?

The 'why stay?' question is also asked by those who never have been or no longer are part of the Christian church. In these instances I hear the question differently again. From those who have no vested interest in defending Christianity as they perceive it, comes clarity of vision in respect to the women within. It is in the nature of the 'outsider' status to be able to see, sometimes, what 'insiders' cannot see. The absurdity of some of the attitudes in church towards women is easily apparent to outsiders. Those of us within would do well on occasion to try and see ourselves as they do.

And yet, here too, I hesitate about the question. For despite all the ambiguity inherent to groups of people struggling to be faithful to Christ, such communities embody a reality of faith that cannot be dismissed so easily. This, also, is why I have written this book. For the insights of those not within the church, while frequently valid, are not the whole truth of Christian experience. To see for the first time or to know deeply within yourself, as a woman, your own subordination in your faith can be severely disturbing; indeed, to the extent that it seems impossible to remain a person of faith at all. Therefore, while making plain the mechanisms of women's subordination, I also indicate how this is not essential to the outworking of Christian faith. For Christian tradition has within it the vision and resources for the affirmation of women's full humanity.

The 'why stay?' question has other meaning when women ask it of themselves. In their struggle for integrity and belonging, their search for self-hood yet self-transcendence, many women subject themselves to rigorous scrutiny as they try to make sense of their lives as female Christians. Often this is a lonely struggle, with few tools readily available and little company along the way. The 'answers' to the question that these women could give do not come from the perspective of either the deflectors or the observing outsiders. They come from those who inhabit the reality of their own existence as women of Christian faith striving for their own authentic personhood. We may ask who is posing the 'why stay?' question, but is anyone listening to the answers?

I am not claiming, in the following pages, to be speaking for all women in the sense that the argument in this book is held by all women. It is, however, a feminist analysis of women's Christian experience, offered for all women (and indeed men). I do not believe that because many women do not recognise their own subordination it makes it any less real. Therefore, this book is no abstract exercise. My advocacy of a feminist engagement with Christian faith is not for the sake of argument, but for the sake of women.

Chapter 1

WOMEN'S WORLD:
Faith, feminism and women's experience

> *Mary has chosen the better part, which will not be taken away from her.*
>
> Jesus of Nazareth

The gospel of Luke tells a story of Jesus' visit to the home of a woman named Martha (Luke 10:38 – 42). In this familiar but, as I shall suggest, frequently misread passage, Martha and her sister Mary respond to their encounter with Jesus in different ways. While Martha is depicted as 'distracted' away from Jesus, Mary is clearly focused on their guest, listening to his every word. Unhappy with her sister's behaviour, Martha voices her objection with Jesus. He, however, affirms Mary's action, describing it as her choice of 'the better part', which will not be taken away from her.

These words, as I elaborate below, are not a devaluing of practical concerns (an assumption derived from the criticism of Martha). Nor are they a rationale for women's submission and passivity (an idea drawn from the approval of the actions of Mary). Rather they are a profound challenge to those theologies, religious practices and social norms that inhibit or diminish women's full human personhood. And they are an affirmation of women's entitlement to enjoy the fullness of life offered in Christian experience.

In this story we, along with Martha and Mary, are confronted with the implications of faith, of responding to the good news that 'the kingdom of God has come near', of working out what God's liberation means in our lives and society.[1] Later I shall suggest that it is because Martha sees the challenge to social norms and place that she hesitates in her faith commitment, at least in this instance of encounter with Jesus. As we shall also see, her hesitation does not last. When we come to this text, however, we come with the legacy of two millennia of understanding and experience that has shaped and moulded Christian faith. Our situation is one where women are not properly valued and fully included within Christianity. Women are valued and included in some ways, but not in ways that sufficiently do justice to either the authenticity of the new life in the kingdom of God or to women who belong to God's kingdom and to whom the kingdom belongs. Therefore, for us, Jesus' promise and affirmation becomes a question: how, in the way we understand and experience Christian faith today, is there the threat or actuality of women's diminishment, of something being taken away that is properly theirs? And what can be done to restore to women their full personhood? This is what this book is about. It brings feminist questions to bear on Christian faith.

EXCLUSION AND INVISIBILITY

Of course, this is not the usual way that this passage is applied. Typically this story has been understood to be teaching the importance of the contemplative, sometimes called 'spiritual', lifestyle represented by Mary in comparison to the practical one, which is portrayed by Martha. This interpretation was mentioned a number of times by the women whose voices appear in this book. A Presbyterian woman in her early fifties said about this text: 'I've looked at that story so often.

I'm very aware that I'm a Martha and I would like to be a Mary.' When asked what she meant by a 'Martha', she said, 'A person who's busy in the kitchen, getting everything done, and fussing round, and everything has to be right. And the challenge is the life of Mary who was able to sit quietly at the feet of the Lord.'

There are two consequences of this reading of the text. The first is that the text has become seen as a 'woman's text', something usually kept for women-focused services and events, because it is understood as referring to a female dilemma of balancing domestic duties with personal devotion. This is actually more of a twentieth-century, Western, white, middle-class reading of the text than a reading that would be applicable to women everywhere, but it is nevertheless the most common understanding and use of it in the West. It is rare to have this text preached to a mixed gathering with the 'practical versus the spiritual' as a dilemma facing men in their lives, let alone used to address an all-male gathering. It is as if these several verses of Scripture are simply overlooked for the church as a whole because it is assumed that with women as central characters in a domestic setting it cannot possibly apply to men or mixed gatherings. This despite the fact that Old Testament narratives of men in militaristic settings at war, for example, are frequently expounded upon as a means whereby both men and women might learn something of God.

In this treatment of a biblical text we see one of the insights that feminism brings to Christian faith, namely its androcentric nature – the way our religious expression centres around and develops out of male experience and understanding, excluding and making invisible female experience and understanding. Put another way, humanity is defined descriptively and normatively in terms of men. Hence, the assumption that lessons from male biblical characters have something of relevance to say to all of humanity, both women and men, but female biblical characters only have something to say for women. This male dominance, however, gives a false understanding of reality for 'only half the story has been told'.[2] What is more, an androcentric world view sees men as 'the bearers of authority, power and value to the relative or complete exclusion of women'.[3] In the church it is men who have interpreted the Bible and Christian tradition, formulated and applied Christian doctrine, conducted acts of worship, established hierarchies of power, and inhabited pulpits and governing bodies. An androcentric framework has affected not only our social arrangements, but the way we speak of God, the way we speak of each other, and the way we organise ourselves in church institutions.

AN IMPOSSIBLE BURDEN

The second consequence of the usual reading of this text, which is related to the first, is that a division is created between the spiritual and the material. In this division, or dualism, the spiritual is considered of worth, valuable and most important, with physical and material embodiment seen as its opposite and, therefore, of little worth, value and importance. Read this way the text presents a choice to be made between the spiritual and the material with the correct choice clearly understood as the spiritual option, which consequently devalues material needs and concerns and all those who deal with the material.

This consequence is related to it being seen as a woman's text because so often in the mind-set that makes such divisions between the spiritual and the material, women are associated with the latter. Much of women's lives focus around caring and responsibility for domestic needs as well as their particular physicality, which involves bearing children. Applied in this way the story becomes an impossible burden for anyone but particularly for women. How do you achieve personal piety, which is understood as something separate from practical involvement, when much of your life inevitably consists of attention to material necessities? It is also ironic that a church which generally relies on its women as 'Martha's' to function in terms of the practicalities of its corporate life (cleaning, church-decoration, child-care, catering, and so forth) should at the same time urge them to be 'Mary's', prioritising personal prayerful devotion above all else.

Into this dualism of the spiritual and the material comes a further contribution from feminism, which has shown the damage that such a division has done in the lives of women. For along with the devaluing of women's contribution to our material existence, there is the dissociation of female human embodiment from that which is spiritual and consequently the alienation of women from the divine. In other words, because women are associated so strongly with physicality, in particular their role in reproduction, and because in an androcentric interpretation of human existence this physicality is seen as belonging to the material realm, it is viewed as incompatible with spiritual realities. In short, maleness is seen as more akin to divinity than femaleness. An obvious outworking of this is women's exclusion from priesthood, but it is apparent also in the dominant use of male language and imagery to talk of God. And it is evident in ideas about women's nature as passive rather than active, which effectively subordinate women to men in hierarchies of power, whether in church, home or society.

All of this is in contrast to the association of maleness with the spiritual and, hence, men's suitability to represent the divine not only in terms of image but also in terms of status and action. In other words, it supports a patriarchal social order. Referring to societies where the rule of the father is the basic principle of social organisation within both the family and society as a whole, the patriarchal system has 'shaped the cultural symbolism of classical societies and their religious expressions'.[4] The influence of this has been to structure both social systems and the cultural symbols about the nature of reality (that is, theology) into 'a hierarchy of male over female, father over sons, master over slaves (servants)'.[5]

The injustice of this male dominance and female subordination is reflected in the term 'women's oppression'. Serene Jones has described women's oppression as the 'dynamic forces, both personal and social, that diminish or deny the flourishing of women'.[6] While oppression is frequently associated with the injustice embedded in social systems, it is also evident in theology that has been used to diminish or distort women's sense of who they are. The systemic nature of oppression, that is, the way women's subordination is part and parcel of the way we think and behave, means that we do not always recognise it for what it is. We are used to the way things are. For this reason, sometimes people play a part in perpetuating women's oppression without an awareness that they are doing so. Any woman who has tried to have a conversation in the church about using gender inclusive language rather than male language and has met with great resistance to even the suggestion that this is important, will understand how ingrained ideas about male dominance are.

While women as well as men may lack awareness of the nature and mechanisms of women's oppression, because women live the subordinated reality they often have an understanding that men do not have. In other words, because women experience the disadvantage, marginalisation and inequality of unjust gender relations, they are more aware of it than men, who do not inhabit this reality. Put another way, male power and privilege prevent men from understanding women's real social and structural position. Feminist theory calls this subordinated experience of women a feminist standpoint,[7] which, because it is a lived experience, 'is not simply an interested position (interpreted as bias) but is interested in the sense of being engaged'.[8] The strength of a feminist standpoint is its ability to unmask the real circumstances of women's lives in order to bring about a change in their situation. Much empirical work by feminists has concentrated on exploring women's reality (in all its diversity) demonstrating the nature and mechanisms of their subordination. This is part of what I do in this book in considering the lives of Christian women. As Alison Webster states, 'what matters in assessing the impact of Christianity upon women's lives is how they have experienced Christianity . . . For the impact of Christianity is not felt in the realm of the abstract and theoretical, but in concrete reality.'[9] In making visible and giving voice to women's own experience in terms of their social, cultural, physical and political realities, it is possible to identify the ways in which women have been excluded, marginalised and undervalued, and hence, to begin to find ways to put right that which is wrong, unjust, unkind or wasteful.

Sometimes because women's subordination is so pervasive, we may think that it is inevitable, even 'natural', simply because it is the way it has always been. With this thinking it is difficult to envision new ways of being, or to find new sources of hope. Into this context of oppression we need liberation to come. Lisa Isherwood suggests that for liberation to be a 'meaningful word we need to imagine another reality can exist, one in which there is no need for oppression'.[10] With this in mind, we return to our gospel narrative.

LIBERATING READING

When we become aware of the oppressive framework that has influenced the traditional interpretation of the story, we may look at it afresh to find some meaning that is consistent with rather than contradictory of Jesus' liberating message of the good news of the coming of God's kingdom. Seeing these verses in the context that Luke has carefully placed them provides the first clue. It is often presented that this incident took place on one of the occasions that Jesus was visiting his friends Martha and Mary. From John's gospel we know how deeply Jesus cared for Mary, Martha and their brother Lazarus. They are described as those whom Jesus loved (John 11:3, 5) and Jesus weeps when he meets the grieving sisters after Lazarus' death (John 11:35). There is the sense that Jesus spent some time with these people and had established good relationships with them. Therefore, against that general knowledge, when we come to this event in Martha's home, we tend to think of it as one of the occasions Jesus was visiting. However, the text itself suggests that this was in fact a new encounter being recorded here: 'Now as they went on their way, he entered a certain village, where a woman named Martha welcomed him into her home' (Luke 10:38).

Indeed this incident comes at the end of two chapters which focus on Jesus' mission not just to the Jewish nation (the mission of the twelve) but to the whole world (the mission of the seventy). Jesus instructs the seventy on how they should conduct themselves as they go about proclaiming the good news. He sends them to towns where he himself intended to go. They were to go and stay where they were welcomed, receiving the hospitality of one house rather than moving about, and were to minister to that town in return. Jesus also says that whoever listens to these disciples listens to him, and whoever rejects them rejects him and the one who sent him (Luke 10:1 – 11).

In this encounter with Martha and her sister Mary we see these things happening. Hospitality is given by Martha, Jesus spoke, and Mary listened. Therefore it is more likely that what we have here is a story of the first encounter with Jesus in person by Martha and Mary, the start of their relationship with him, the beginning of their discipleship of Jesus.[11] Within this, however, the two aspects of hospitality and listening seem to be divided. Martha provides the hospitality and Mary does the listening. Both of these need further examination.

It is not necessarily correct to assume that this was a select gathering of just Jesus, Martha and Mary. While other people are not mentioned as being there, there are other occasions where, while only one character is mentioned, it becomes apparent that others were present (see Luke 2:4, 5; 7:6, 9; Matthew 12:46 – 50). We know Jesus did not usually travel alone. In addition to the twelve who were nearly his constant companions, there were the seventy and Luke also mentions several women, some named, who travelled with Jesus providing for him out of their own resources (Luke 8:2 – 3; Mark 15:40f also makes mention of these and other women). So the picture we have is of a larger group than the twelve, consisting of both women and men, who travelled with Jesus and were his disciples. Frequently in the gospels, where there are stories of Jesus sharing a meal in homes, he is accompanied by his followers.

The composition of those present with Jesus in Martha's home helps in understanding what is happening here. If there were a number of people present it could explain Martha's preoccupation with her 'many tasks'. The exact nature of these tasks is not specified but the phrase used indicates household chores. Martha is described as *distracted* by these many tasks (not busy or over burdened).[12] The sense is of her being dragged or pulled away from something else, which in this case is listening to the teachings of Jesus, which is what Mary was doing.

Mary is described as 'sitting at the feet of Jesus', an idiom Luke also records on the lips of Paul when he says of himself that he sat at the feet of Gamaliel (Acts 22:3). In other words, he was a disciple of the rabbi Gamaliel and he learnt at the feet of his teacher. Mary is depicted here as actively taking on the role of the disciple. This is not simply a passive, polite listening, but the kind of engaged listening that is involved in being a follower of Jesus and which leads to an active response. Earlier Luke describes the Gerasene man healed of his demons as sitting at the feet of Jesus, clothed and in his right mind. He then leaves Jesus proclaiming to everyone what Jesus had done (Luke 8:26 – 39). His listening is followed by an active response. The personal piety for women which is so often read from these verses is usually understood as quietness, reflection and even submissiveness. Yet while listening is involved, discipleship is always active. It is about both hearing and doing the word of God (Luke 8:21). The enormous political implications of this become apparent as the story of the early church unfolds. Discipleship then, for many women as well as men, had the consequence of imprisonment. In Acts Saul is described as 'ravaging the church by entering house after house; dragging off both men and women, he committed them to prison' (Acts 8:3). The interpretation of this passage in Luke in regard to personal piety has more to do with a particular understanding of womanhood as quiet, demure and passive than with the text itself.

Jesus' response to Martha's appeal to him for Mary's help sheds more light on what is being talked about here. Jesus, in a way that is not unkind to Martha,[13] affirms Mary's action of listening to him. Kenneth Bailey considers that Martha was concerned not about the practicalities of how she would show appropriate hospitality for her visitor(s), but about the implications of what Mary was doing, having joined a group with men and become a disciple of the rabbi Jesus. To a cultural insider, he suggests, the real communication taking place would be 'crystal clear'.[14] He imaginatively gives voice to the kind of concerns Martha would have had: 'The other rabbis don't have women disciples! What's happening under my nose is outrageous and unprecedented! What will the neighbors think and what will the local rabbis say? Imagine – my sister – a disciple of a rabbi! If she continues she will be involved in daily interaction with *young unmarried* men! Who will marry the poor girl after this? Her reputation will be ruined! She'll *listen* to *you* Jesus! You *must* tell her that her place is here in the kitchen with me!'[15] Therefore, Jesus' response to Martha being 'worried and distracted by many things' acknowledges that she is not simply concerned over having additional domestic help at that particular moment, but about the implications of Mary's action, which challenges accepted gender norms. However, Jesus affirms that Mary has chosen what is needed, the better part or portion, a reference often to food, as she is feeding from himself, he who is the living bread who can give living water to drink so you need never be thirsty again.[16]

In this reading these verses say something about the kingdom of God and its ramifications *in* material realities rather than being about a dualistic split *between* the spiritual and the material. These material realities include our social systems as well as our physical embodiment. To pursue this further it is worth thinking about how Luke's readers would have been receiving this story. When this passage is used with groups of women the response is often that many feel sympathy with Martha, and can understand her responsibilities. It does seem reasonable that Martha should have had some help, whether you view this in terms of the traditional women's role or simply from the point of view that hospitality involves such practicalities that have to be provided by someone. In other words, on hearing this story for the first time, the readers would hear it from Martha's point of view. Compare this to the previous verses and the parable Jesus tells of the good Samaritan. Our over-familiarity with that story as with so many of Jesus' parables which are set in such a different context to our own, means we have lost the subversive impact that these stories had in their original context. But isn't it possible that in the same way people were amazed that it was the Samaritan who acts as someone who loves God and not the religious elite, people would have been surprised that it was Mary whom Jesus commends and defends and not Martha? In the same way that previously held racial prejudices are upset in the kingdom of God as the parable of the good Samaritan would have shouted out to its first hearers, so are matters of socialised gender role and place. This kingdom upsets so many rules and norms: it is for Gentiles as well as Jews, it is fully for women as well as men, it supersedes kinship networks (Luke 14:26; Matthew 12:46 – 50). It is a new way of thinking, of living, of behaving, of relating.

Understood in this manner this is a passage about the revolutionary discipleship that is called for which transforms our ways of thinking and behaving. It is not about spirituality narrowly defined and understood as being more important than material concerns. The kingdom of God involves material needs; after all, Jesus is looked after by those around him. It is because certain women provided for him out of their own resources that Peter and others were able to leave their nets and follow Jesus (Luke 8:2 – 3). This is not a gendered division of response. The woman Jesus met at the well in John's gospel, in similar fashion to the fishermen, left her water jar to go and tell others about Jesus (John 4:28). The kingdom of God disturbs our established ways in all things that have kept us in bondage. It is liberation for the captives (Luke 4:18). It is the *one thing* needed and affects *everything* else.

Read this way, the story is about what it means for people and communities to respond to the gospel. While it speaks in a special way to women, affirming God's liberating action in their lives, it has something to say to everyone. It is a profound challenge to the inequality currently embedded in gender relationships. For, as feminism has emphasised, changes for the better in the lives of women cannot operate in isolation from the rest of society. This is why what is a promise for some is such a threat to others who face the disturbance of a system that has provided them privilege or protection. For if those who are discriminated against are to find a new freedom, then those who have practised injustice must let go of their power. If those who are excluded are to be included, then those who want to keep others out must change. If those on the margins are to be brought in from the outside, the centre will look very different. And if those who are undervalued are to have their worth recognised, it will mean a new value system for everyone. The task of ending women's subordination, therefore, involves creating something new. It is not only about the absence of the bad, but the presence of what is good. Take, for example, the notion of equality. While equality tends to be associated with legislative measures and regulations that remove discrimination, it is far more. In the words of Marcia

Riggs, 'Equality . . . refers to relationships that empower groups of people who have been considered unequal on the basis of differences, such as race, gender, and class.'[17] It is such an empowering of women that affirms their 'full and equivalent humanity'[18] that would be a concrete expression of God's liberation and which is not to be taken away from them.

PARTICULAR WOMEN

The notion of empowering groups who have been considered unequal on the basis of differences such as race and class, as well as gender, draws attention to the diversity inherent in women's experience of subordination. In other words, while a gender system operates discriminating against women on the basis of their sex, there are differences among women themselves, and these differences have their own, yet frequently related, systems of oppression and injustice. Take the reflection of a Catholic woman in Northern Ireland who spent some time working in South Africa during the Apartheid regime. She spoke of the 'realisation that blacks and coloured people were others and connecting that with my feeling of second-class citizenship in Northern Ireland at the time I was growing up. And then being caught in this because my white skin made me first-class and yet my life experience up to then . . . was second-class and this torn feeling – and I struggled with that the whole time I was there.'

It is the existence of such differences that has challenged the idea of a feminist standpoint — is it possible to talk of women's experience of subordination as if it were one thing? The recognition of differences among women has led to speaking of feminist standpoints in the plural, as this acknowledges the many forms of women's subordination. It is necessary also to see the connections between different kinds of oppression. Elisabeth Schüssler Fiorenza, for example, has coined the word 'kyriarchy', from the Greek meaning rule or dominion of the master, in order to investigate the interlocking structures of systemic oppression involving not only gender but also race, colonialism, class, culture, religion and 'other discursive formations of domination'.[19] In any society, she maintains, these work together not in terms of additions of oppression and discrimination, but their interaction produces a multiplication of effect and consequence.

The existence of many forms of oppression does not undermine the injustice of any one form. The value of feminist standpoints, that is, making women's experiences of oppression (their exclusion, exploitation, undervaluing, undermining) crucial for understanding and action, is the focus it gives to opposing women's subordination in particular situations. At the same time, this must always be done in awareness of other injustices that are faced by women in different situations. Judith Plaskow and Carol Christ comment that 'although this may seem paradoxical, it is often through the personal, through the articulation of particularity and what seems to be difference, that connection and universality are suddenly revealed. Indeed, one of the early insights of feminist theology was that, like a good novel, poem, or play, theology best illumines the universal in human experience through attention to the details of human life.'[20]

In this book I explore the reality of Christian women's experience with both its current subordination and its hope of God's liberation, through the particularities of women in Northern Ireland.

Northern Ireland is a place where Christian religious affiliation (at 85 per cent)[21] and church involvement (at 61 per cent)[22] remain high. Christianity continues to be an integral part of life for many people. Church connections and religious ideologies not only directly affect women involved in the various denominations, but also play a part in influencing, 'sometimes unconsciously, the values and perceptions of an even wider circle of women'.[23] Generally the churches have been so widely influential in Northern Ireland that it is hard 'to disentangle their role from that of the other institutions of society'.[24] In part, this is because of the enmeshment of national and religious identity that so pervades the narrative of Northern Ireland. Religion is suffused with further meaning in a context where disputed nationality claims, along with their associated culture and history, align closely with differing religious affiliations.

While its religious profile is often perceived in terms of 'bipolar religious monoliths', that is, Catholics and Protestants, there is a 'complexity of religious commitment and experience' that exists in Northern Ireland.[25] There is a theological spectrum ranging from liberal to evangelical or fundamentalist within Protestantism that runs across the denominations.[26] John Whyte concludes that while the Protestant Catholic divide is greater than that between liberal and fundamentalist, if religion was the sole cause of conflict in Northern Ireland, one might expect there to be more than two communities.[27] It is also true that within Catholicism there exist differing theological opinions. Such diversity is reflected in the 55 women whose voices appear in this book. Aged between twenty-one and seventy-three at the time of interview[28] and based throughout Northern Ireland, these women come from a range of theological outlooks as well as denominational affiliation.[29]

In terms of church institutions, the four largest denominations in Northern Ireland are the Catholic Church in Ireland[30] (40 per cent of the population), the Presbyterian Church in Ireland (21 per cent), the Church of Ireland (15 per cent), and the Methodist Church in Ireland (four per cent).[31] I refer to these in shortened form as Catholic, Presbyterian and Methodist while recognising that for the latter two there are other denominations in Ireland that also have these terms in their titles.[32] For the Church of Ireland, to avoid any ambiguity, I use the term Anglican, which reflects its world-wide connection with the Anglican Communion. Organisationally each of these four denominations covers the whole of Ireland, North and South, having been founded before the political division of Ireland in 1922. Forty-four of the women interviewed belong to one of these four denominations. Eleven come from other Protestant groups including Baptist, Reformed Presbyterian, Elim Pentecostal, and non-denominational fellowships. Given the small numbers interviewed from each of these groups, in order to maintain their anonymity, I refer to these women as Protestant.

The women talked about their Christian faith experience, in particular their understanding of God, their understanding of themselves, their relationship to church institutions, and some of their life experiences. While a few of the women openly identified themselves as feminist, others were obviously uncomfortable being seen in this way. As is true elsewhere, general support for women's equality is not connected to an embrace of feminism. There is a widespread resistance (and in some cases notable hostility) to feminism and frequently expressed desire on the part of many women in churches not to be labelled as feminist, a term around which there is considerable suspicion. One of its main associations is that it is incompatible with Christianity. One woman told how she had deliberately 'let go' of many of the issues around being a woman in church because most feminists ended up outside of the church and she did not want to. This book addresses this dilemma. In the following chapters, as someone who owns both a feminist and a Christian identity, I consider the nature and mechanisms of Christian women's subordination.

The way we talk of God and its impact on women is explored in chapter two. How Christian women come to understand and value themselves is considered in chapter three. Chapter four addresses women's social and physical embodiment as wives and mothers, examining how ideologies and practices around these states affect all women whether or not they are married or have children. Chapter five investigates women's experience within church institutions. The interlocking nature of multiple forms of oppression is the subject of chapter six, along with issues around power and powerlessness when exploring women's experience of community conflict. These themes also relate to each other across the chapters. For example, women's own experience as mothers and their community engagement addresses how we might speak of God, and women's sense of value and personal identity have something to say about how we function both as a society and as Christian communities. In all of this I use resources from feminist thinking, feminist theology, Christian tradition and women's experience in order to see the manner in which women have been denied the 'better part', God's liberation, and how what has been taken away can be redeemed.

A final word in this chapter about the women with whom it began. When we meet Martha in John's gospel, we see that her hesitation in embracing the new life that Jesus offered did not last. It is Martha who leaves her house to greet Jesus when she hears he is near and Martha who declares, like Peter, that Jesus is the Messiah, the Son of God, the one coming into the world (John 11:20, 27). In her, as in Mary, is the hope of God's liberation. Our task is to work out what God's liberation means for us in our generation.

Chapter 2

GOD IN WHOSE IMAGE?:
The dominance of male God-talk

[Is God male?] Yes, because he created man first in his – oh well, good question! I thought because he created man in his likeness and then he created woman but I suppose, I don't know, I don't have any other backing up for that. I suppose the next question then is, is he white or black? Yes I do [think God is male], but as with an awful lot of things in my Christian life at the moment, an awful lot of it is because what I've been taught and what I've learned, taking the word of other people and only now am I really looking into it and reading it myself and learning.

Protestant woman in her twenties

I feel that a male God and the way that we teach an all-male God is excluding women, you know, I do feel that . . . If we see only the higher power, the God, the good, the decision-maker, you know, as all-male, then I think that that devalues women.

Catholic woman in her twenties

'OK let's start with a big question!' one woman replied when asked how she would describe God. She is right. Talking about God is a big question. The idea and experience of God is the essence of Christian faith, understanding, and practice. What is more, our beliefs and feelings about God cannot be kept separate from the rest of our lives. For bound up in our understanding of God is the meaning we give to our own existence: our hopes, fears and dreams; our identity and sense of belonging; our values and life choices; our relationships with others; and our place in the world. All of this human experience mirrors how we understand and relate to God. But, at the same time, it also contributes to how we experience and speak of God. In other words, our sense of God impacts our lives, whether we acknowledge this or not, and has the potential both for good and harm. As Elizabeth Johnson repeatedly says in the opening pages in her book considering God, 'The symbol of God functions.'[1] To reflect on our understanding of God is, therefore, vital.

In particular, how we speak of God both communicates and shapes this understanding. How in our God-talk is Christian women's personhood diminished or denied with the resulting theological, ecclesiological and social subordinated reality, and what is required for it to be restored? Or put another way, how does the way we speak of God discriminate against women in church and society? And what can we do to change this? For as we shall see, our God-talk is not neutral in its effects upon our lives as women and men.

TALKING OF GOD

'God is faithful, always faithful', said a young Anglican woman, 'and completely just and holy. All encompassing, everywhere, too big for words really. Close but still like really, like mega superior and yet I guess it's the paradox . . . he is a father and I can tell him everything but sometimes I'm just like in awe of him . . . like a really good, good person to have on your side.' In using many different terms, even some that appear contradictory, her words are typical of the way the women in this book spoke of God. For what was most striking about their descriptions was the variety of expressions they used.

While the term father was mentioned the most times, only five women offered father as an exclusive term for thinking about God and it does not emerge as the singular image that encapsulates God for the majority of the women. God as creator or God's creating activity was mentioned as was God as friend, along with other personal images of spirit, mother, parent, Jesus/Christ, judge, lord, and king. There were also impersonal images and concepts, for example: the notion of God as big, 'I don't know who God is apart from huge'; God in nature, 'When I'm out sailing I feel the power of creation and appreciate that it's God'; God as a presence, 'I think that God is an immense presence that is intimately connected with every atom that's around me and in me.' There were frequent references to aspects of God's nature and/or behaviour, including mercy, justice, forgiveness, holiness, sovereignty, love, nurture, comfort, concern, healing, protection, God as almighty, powerful, good, omnipotent, wise, life-giving, infinite, steadfast, faithful, generous. Indeed the most common way women talked of God was in these kind of relational terms, that is, in terms of their understanding of God's activity toward them. As one woman said, 'I can't think of him apart from what he's like.'

A mixture of these images of God and God's activities was usually presented by the women in their attempts at articulating their sense and understanding of the divine. As a Presbyterian woman commented, 'He is that father figure and yet as well he's the Lord and the Creator and it's this combination which is so fascinating, I suppose.'

What these many ways of speaking of God vividly remind us is that there is an inherent dilemma in speaking about God. How do we encompass in finite, human language that which is infinite, divine and in some manner at least, if not as traditionally understood in terms of remoteness or dispassion, transcends human experience? In the words of an Anglican woman: 'As soon as you start to put words on [God] you're making it finite or something.' This does not mean that it is not possible to talk of God. But it does indicate the need for an awareness that our language for God is metaphorical. That is to say, we take words about things with which we are familiar and imaginatively apply them to God, even though they are not literal descriptions, that is, the words are not being used in their 'primary, matter-of-fact sense'.[2] So the psalmist talks of God as a rock to describe his experience of God and not to mean that God is a mineral (Psalm 31:2 – 3). Boaz speaks of Ruth taking refuge under God's wings, but he does not infer that God is a bird (Ruth 2:12). We may call God father to describe our relationship with God, but not to indicate that the divine is a human male. We talk of being born of God in order to try and describe the spiritual reality of the life we have in God while not meaning that God is a birthing mother. We use images to put into words our understanding and experience of God, all the time remembering that, while they may be sufficient for that task at any given moment, these images are not literal definitions of God. Inherent in the idea of metaphor is the sense that God both *is* and *is not* like the image used when attempting to convey something of the divine. Put another way, God-talk is 'language of comparison and not of identification'.[3]

If we forget that any particular description of God is a metaphor, that is, an imaginative rather than literal form of speech, the danger is that the image becomes equated with the divine itself and not simply pointing to the divine. We know that it is possible for material objects, such as statues, to be seen this way, but so can ideas and concepts, such as God as king or father. As Gail Ramshaw comments, 'refusing to examine our engraved speech leads to an idolatry more sophisticated but no less culpable than that with the golden calf.'[4] A metaphor for God is more likely to become idolatrous if it is used habitually, singularly or dominantly, with the familiar and near exclusive usage eroding our awareness of its figurative nature.

To equate any such image with God is, of course, an injustice to the divine. But it also holds inherent dangers for human beings. If through the habitual, over- or near-exclusive use of a particular image or concept, however valid it may be in its potential to provide some understanding of God, its metaphorical nature is forgotten, it easily becomes understood as a dominant or defining way of speaking of God. In particular, when that image or series of images are overwhelmingly male, to the extent that talk of God in female terms produces great objection and even revulsion, then there are consequences for the way we live as women and men together in church and society. For if God is male, men stand in a different relationship to God than do women, and there is a difference in the social standing women and men have relative to each other. A God – man – woman hierarchy results in which men become the mediators between women and God, and men rule over women with divine authority.

Perhaps one way to safeguard against such idolatry in our expressions for the divine is to use many images for God. However, while most of the women in this book spoke of God in many different ways, their God-talk, as we shall see, is not immune from the influence of metaphorical language about God becoming understood as definitions of God.

MALE GOD-TALK

The near-exclusive use of male images for God within Christian tradition, practice and popular thinking means that the idea of the maleness of God pervades the many ways women talk of God, even in their use of impersonal terms and talk of God's activity. And it does so in a way that has an impact not only on ideas about God, but on the concrete reality of women's lives.

God as male

Although Christian belief is that God *created* male and female but is not in Godself male and female, in practice a different understanding often pervades our consciousness and practice. As Elizabeth Johnson says, 'While officially it is rightly and consistently said that God is spirit and so beyond identification with either male or female sex, yet the daily language of preaching, worship, catechesis, and instruction conveys a different message: God is male, or at least more like a man than a woman, or at least more fittingly addressed as male than as female.'[5]

When asked directly if she thought that God was male an older Presbyterian woman replied, 'I think God is male, yes I think so . . . I think it's my age and my upbringing, you know. I would be prepared to listen, you know, and quite enjoy discussion about that but yes, I think I think God is male.' Altogether 20 women stated they believed God was male, some with quick and sure responses, others taking time to think but nevertheless in agreement that God was male. 'I think he is yes, yes', said a Protestant woman, 'I've never thought of him as female. I've thought of him as tender and loving, but not as female. He's my heavenly father.'

In contrast, 16 women were clear that God was not male. 'I can't understand why people want to confine God to any human terms whatsoever. It's crazy,' a Catholic woman stated. 'The idea of containing God within male figure or female figure would be anathema at present,' explained another woman, 'I mean it's so restrictive.'

A further group of women expressed the view that God had no gender or was above gender. As one Protestant woman put it, 'It's like saying is he Irish, you know. You can't talk about God in those terms.'

Yet despite this variety of understanding, all but four women used 'he', 'his', or 'him', either frequently or at some point in referring to God, indicating the prevalence of masculine terminology for God. As one woman reflected: 'We're so finite we have to boil it down to something we can conceptualise. So I suppose that's how he's ended up male, there's me saying he. Because we've only got he, she and it and they and I suppose we can't say they even though we think of God as plural including Jesus and the Holy Spirit. We're relating one to one so we do need a singular pronoun. We need an extra one.'

In fact, the dominance of male imagery for God makes it difficult to think of God in terms other than male. A Catholic woman recognised this when she observed, 'Well he's obviously portrayed as male, you know, but . . . being God I'd say he's male with all the feminine qualities, if you know what I mean. He's always been portrayed as male so I can't think of him as anything else.' Another woman concurs: 'It's really difficult because I really don't believe that [God is male] and a lot of the ways I think about God are actually genderless, but I grew up with a male Presbyterian God, you know, and it's not easy to shake off.'

Such pervasive male imagery works at a deep level even when women's own belief is that God is not male. So a Protestant woman commented, 'I suppose when you sit down and analyse the Bible and stuff, God really doesn't have a gender but yes, in my mind, God's male.' Despite the fact that 'intellectually . . . God is neither male or female', another woman went on to say, 'but having said that, you know, the father image has been stressed so much and used so much that I think it's hard to not sometimes think of God as male'. Similarly for another interviewee: 'I know, right, from my teaching, that God is spirit, right. But yes I think of him as male, but I'm sure that's a product of my upbringing. I was just brought up that God is our father, you know, the Father-God, Jesus the Son and the Holy Spirit. So automatically . . . when I think of God I think of father.'

It is not only that God is spoken and thought of as male, regardless of a clear belief that God is not to be equated with human gender. The entrenchment of the idea of God as male also means that women can have difficulty in conceiving of God using female terms, whether or not they hold a view of God as including or being beyond gender. So for a Catholic woman, 'I either think of God as not having a sex or male but not female.' Another spoke of how she was 'more comfortable with a male image of God . . . I find it difficult to see God as female or having no sex at all'.

In addition to having difficulty in thinking of God in female imagery, women also may be opposed to doing so. In responding to the question if she thought God was male a Presbyterian woman reflected, 'I don't really think that God is either [male or female] but I suppose a more honest answer would be to say yes. But it certainly doesn't matter to me . . . I wouldn't want to hear anybody talk about God as her. Now maybe that indicates that I do think of God as male.' A Methodist woman commented that she didn't 'think of gender in relation to God at all . . . No I don't see him as strictly male.' However, she went on to say, 'but equally I would find it offensive to say he was female because that's [*pause*] that's different . . . If you say God is a woman that has got something aggressive in it to me, aggressive feminism and I don't like that.' When asked what were the implications of saying God is male, she replied, 'That's just traditional, it's only traditional, it's not aggressively male, or masculine, it's only historical.'

This resistance to female metaphorical God-talk emphasises the overwhelming influence that male God-talk has had within Christian tradition. That female imagery should feel at a deep psychic level so incongruent with the idea of God while male imagery does not, is not, contrary to the Methodist woman, simply historical and (part of) the tradition. Such imagery is masculine and is aggressively male. It effectively serves to subordinate women in a God – male – female hierarchy because its pervasive use conveys that femaleness is not a suitable metaphorical vehicle for speaking of the divine.

Femaleness has not simply been left out of our God-talk, as if by oversight or accident. Rather, it has been deliberately excluded as unfit and incapable of being imaginatively used to express the divine. The reasons for this, as already noted in chapter one, are rooted in dualistic thought[6] which makes a distinction between God and humanity, between spirit and matter, seeing these as mutually exclusive opposites, in hierarchical relationship with the former term being deemed as superior and of greater value than the latter. This framework for understanding the world has influenced both Western philosophical thinking and Christian theology. Maleness and femaleness have been aligned to the basic dualism of God/spirit and humanity/matter. Hence, men were associated with the divine, that which is spiritual, rational, and active, while women were viewed as belonging to the material, that which is natural, emotional and passive, and consequently not considered suitable vehicles with which to speak of God. 'In this profoundly dualistic world view, male is to female as autonomy is to dependence, as strength is to weakness, as fullness is to emptiness, as dynamism is to stasis, as good is to evil. Since the divine principle is pure act and goodness, it necessarily must exclude all dependency, potency, passivity, and prime matter. The logic of this set-up leads inexorably to the conviction that the divine can properly be spoken of only on the model of the spiritually masculine to the exclusion of the passive, material feminine.'[7]

Against this legacy it is perhaps little wonder why female God-talk should feel so wrong to so many people, why, in the words of one woman, 'it's sick the way that . . . all these feminists . . . have to make God female'. She went on to say that such women were 'revealing a lot of insecurities and inadequacies within themselves that it has to be a major issue'. She does not wonder, however, what is being said about women when we argue and feel so deeply that female imagery is anathema to the divine. Before turning to this question, we will consider how the images of God as king, father and Jesus as God incarnate are used to perpetuate male dominance in God-talk and social relations.

God as king

While the image of God as king was mentioned specifically on only a few occasions, the notion of God as a powerful ruler was expressed frequently by the women. 'God . . . is more infinitely powerful than we can ever actually imagine . . . he's a God of incredible power and authority', said a Catholic woman. For a

Presbyterian woman God was 'mighty, powerful, in control. I always find that very important, you know, for me to remember that he's sovereign.' Another Catholic woman expressed this aspect of God in terms of God having 'a plan for all of us. We don't always see it very clearly but . . . it's good for me to know that there's somebody in charge of life, of my life and of the world.'

For a few of these women the idea of God as almighty was associated with fear. As a Presbyterian woman put it, 'I see God . . . as someone who is looking down and watching us – I still have remnants of the fear of God.' In contrast, for other women the idea of God as powerful was comforting: 'I feel that he's in control of all that's going on around us, he's sovereign and he is working out his purposes, if you like, in this world. Some of the things we see happening we're not too happy about, obviously . . . But ultimately I still feel that he is in control and I feel happy about that. I mean, I feel happy that God is there, if you like, in control.'

How is the idea of God as king or ruler used within Christianity to perpetuate women's subordinate position? God portrayed dominantly and in exclusively masculine terms as king, that is, as a male monarch ruling with power over the world, endorses a sense of women's relative powerlessness, dissociates their experience from God-likeness, and, hence, maintains the God – male – female hierarchy. It is not that all women have no power. But the image of God as king, presented in the potent combination of male, powerful and in control (however benevolent), contrasts with the experience of many women as female, powerless and dependent. Speaking of a particular experience in her life very much related to her physical and social identity as a female, one woman commented that this 'put me amongst the powerless and if God is among the powerless you sort of find God there, but you have to give God a different name, you know, because the conventional God doesn't quite fit with the powerless'.

That many women find comfort in the idea of God as

sovereign ruler does not diminish the way this image maintains women's hierarchically subordinated position when it is used dominantly and in exclusively male terms and interpretation. This does not have to be the case however. In the gospels Jesus is portrayed as subverting the notion of kingship from one of power-over-people to service-of-people. So while Jesus spoke of the kingdom of God, which had now come and to which people could belong (see Mark 1:15; 3:35; Luke 10:9), it was a kingdom where the outcasts, powerless and insignificant were welcome, in which the greatest within it was not a tyrannical ruler but a servant of all, and whose king rode humbly on a donkey and was crucified.[8] This use of the metaphor of kingship[9] maintains God's transcendence but does not involve hierarchical dominance that subordinates one sex, race, or group of people to another. In addition, the gospel portrayal of the kingdom of God is a vivid reminder of the nature of metaphorical God-talk: that God is both like and not like, in this instance, a human king. Both power and powerlessness pertain to God. In the words of a Catholic woman, God is 'this immense presence and love and power that leaves itself to powerlessness almost because it's given me free will to be myself'.

Such a combination is only possible, however, when the metaphorical nature of kingship is retained and it ceases to be used either dominantly or amid exclusive male terminology for God.

God as father

While less than half of the women offered the term father in their descriptions of God, when asked specifically how well they related to the notion of God as a father most indicated that it was an image to which they now related positively in some way. For the majority of these women it was a wholly positive response, while others added some qualification to their ownership of the image (for example, the struggle to turn this knowledge into personal experience or an emphasis on also understanding God in other ways). God as father evoked similar meaning to God as king, that is, protection, provision and comfort. In the words of a young Anglican, 'I see God really as a father . . . I value that strength and support and protection and love.' For some women the term father was a negative image, at times echoing the sense of fear that can be bound up in the notion of God as king. A Catholic woman explained, 'I would rather see him as friend and comforter because my relationship with my own father was one of fear and for many years I had a fear of God, you know, he would zap me if I would do anything that was wrong.'

Without doubt, a major component in the understanding of God as father was of God as loving and caring. For a young Protestant woman God as father was considered 'as more of a caring role and who knows best for me and would comfort me, that sort of side, rather than somebody who is unapproachable and [who you're] scared to talk to'. The ideas of a loving yet powerful God were often put together. 'I know God very much as a father', said a young Catholic woman, 'very much as a father, very much as a protector and a provider, but also a God who is more infinitely powerful than we can ever actually imagine with a wisdom that is totally unfathomable.'

Brian Wren has coined this dominant 'metaphor system of divine kingship'[10] KINGAFAP – the King – God – Almighty – Father – Protector – as the themes of protection, fatherliness, kingship and omnipotence are frequently presented together in Christian worship and creeds. In one sense it is difficult to separate the two images of king and father as they interact with each other and indeed both may be understood positively or negatively. However, the image of father is distinctive in that it is more closely related to personal experience than is obviously possible for the model of God as king. Talk of God as father powerfully demonstrates the relationship between images of God and our embodied, situated experience.

For the women in this book it was abundantly clear that the way they related to the image of God as father was firmly dependent upon their own experience of their human fathers, whether this was in a positive, negative or unknown capacity. A Presbyterian woman was happy to make the association of her human father with God: 'I see God as my father, right. Well I had a good father, you know, my earthly father was a good father, so I mean I can identify there that the father figure is someone who cares for you, somebody who looks after you.' A Methodist woman recalled how the notion of God as father had been taught to her. 'I remember so clearly being out in the garden with my father', she said, 'and there must have been some conversation about God because my father said to me, you know, you've got two fathers, you've got me and you've got God and God loves you just the way I do . . . I think that's where my image of God came from.'

The women who responded positively and without qualification to the image of God as a father linked this to good relationships with their own fathers. Those women who did not relate well to this image attributed this to difficult or non-existent father relationships. Put succinctly by a Presbyterian: 'I don't relate at all well to the image of God as father because I have very little conception of what it means to have one.' This consistency of association indicates that for God-talk to be able to speak of God appropriately it must accommodate different human experiences as well as seeking to do justice to the divine. The example of God seen as a father emphasises that we seek to understand God by what we know. This being so we may well conclude that the image of God as mother could be as useful or as much a hindrance in relating to God depending on our own experience. Yet generally this is not the case.

It is not the case because the dominance of male models of God has served to exclude and negate female images and experience to the extent that those things associated with femaleness (whether appropriate or not) have been grafted onto the understanding of God as father. The overwhelming interpretation of the image of God as father was understood as that of caring in terms of provision and nurture. Indeed, for some women, this is what made the image acceptable to them now. A Catholic woman in her thirties explained how 'for years I would have had real problems with [God as father] just in terms of . . . the whole patriarchal system and the way men have in society, you know, [shown] lack of respect of women and everything. But now . . . I do feel that that has changed and . . . there is room for father but not I suppose that father who's watching if you sin or whatever – more sort of a nurturing, supporting father. Not the one that's quite closed or you have to be good for all the time or whatever.'

A more warm affectionate understanding of father has made the image usable to more women. Yet it is still true that while many women identify care and nurture as feminine qualities (see chapter three) which they value, and in some instances see as women's special contribution, when focusing on care and nurture in deity, they do not image the divine in female terms. So, for example, for one woman, caring and nurture become masculine characteristics when applied to God: 'We have to be able to picture [God] some way or another and if the characteristics we are talking about are caring and fathering, you see a lot of that male figure.'

For this woman, caring and fathering are understood almost interchangeably. This association is apparent even when women have come to understand something about God from their *own* experience as a *mother*. A Protestant woman in her fifties spoke of when 'it really slotted into place that God was my father, and that this was an unbreakable relationship, that I never stopped being his daughter. In the same way that whatever my children do they are always my daughters and because of that, you know, they can always come winging home, sure of a welcome. I can visualise some situations where I would find it hard to welcome them, but that wouldn't mean that I would turn them away.' The relationship of comparison on which this woman (and others) draws is understanding God's action towards human beings by reference to her own attitude towards her daughters. In other words, she realises that 'God is to us as I (a *woman*, a *mother*) am to my child'. And yet this does not lead to speaking of God in female terms. God is still father.

It is because of the dominance of male terminology for God that the obvious comparison between some women's own actions as female persons and the actions of God do not lead to female God-talk. Masculine images and male terms for God have become the interpretive framework through which God's activity and even impersonal images have come to be understood. This accounts for the inherent contradiction between women's female experience and their male God-talk. In other words, attributing to God characteristics and modes of behaviour that in human beings they associate as feminine more than masculine, but using exclusively male God-talk.[11] God as father underscores the idea that God is a male authority, albeit for many people a benevolent one.[12] Father as provider/carer (in the same way as God as king or ruler in control) encourages a dependency in women which in concrete terms reinforces women's structurally subordinate position in society and in Christian belief and practice. Anne Thurston puts it like this: 'if we image God as Ruler, King, Almighty Father with dominion over his creatures, are we not reflecting a view of the world which permits some to dominate others? A hierarchical pattern in a religious system or in society means that those on the lowest rungs are always dependent on those above them. If rulers/fathers are benevolent they may thrive; if not, they suffer. To image God solely as Father is dangerous because it can serve to justify social structures which are sustained by power of the strong over the weak.'[13]

The idea of God as father, when understood as male authority, does not encourage female autonomy, that is, women taking active responsibility for their lives in all their relationships. Rather, this understanding of God works against such female agency. As such it provides no incentive to challenge unjust social relations and structures.

Prioritising the use of the image of father for God is said to be supported by Jesus' use of this image. The word Jesus used,

Abba, 'was the intimate word used by children in the family for their fathers. It is not fully conveyed by English terms such as *Daddy*, for it was also a term an adult could use of an older man to signify a combination of respect and affection.'[14] Rosemary Radford Ruether argues that early Christians used the concept of God as Abba 'to liberate the community from human dominance – dependence relationships based on kinship ties or master – servant relationships'.[15] To become part of the kingdom of God is to establish new allegiances and to break old ones. Hence, existing family loyalties (including to parents) are put aside in favour of a new community of brothers and sisters where people are connected not by human kinship blood ties but in belonging to the kingdom of God (see Luke 9:59 – 62; 14:26; Matthew 12:46 – 50). In this new community there is equality and relationships not of dominance and subservience but of friendship (see Matthew 23:1 – 12; John 15:15). Hence, Jesus' use of father subverts the hierarchical model: 'Because God is our king, we need obey no human kings. Because God is our parent, we are liberated from dependence on patriarchal authority.'[16]

While, as Sallie McFague argues, the patriarchal misuse of the image of God as father to endorse male superiority in personal and public life 'is a serious perversion of Jesus' understanding of the father model and utterly opposed to the root-metaphor of Christianity, which is against all worldly hierarchies',[17] the person of Jesus *himself* remains an issue in our imaging of God.

Jesus as God incarnate

The maleness of Jesus both in biblical and other writings is not disputed. The significance of his sex is. The maleness of Jesus is used to imply that maleness is an essential characteristic of divine being itself, or at least that there is more affinity between maleness and divinity than femaleness and the divine.[18] As a Protestant women in her fifties said, 'If our understanding of

God is seen in Jesus, Jesus was male.' In similar vein a Catholic reflected, 'I'm more comfortable with a male image of God and I suppose it's because of Jesus.'

The maleness of Jesus has been given as a reason for the exclusion of women from ordination. It remains a central tenet within Catholicism's exclusively male priesthood. The Catholic priest is the sacramental representative sign of Christ at the Last Supper and on the cross so he must naturally represent what he symbolises – to be a male as Christ was a male. The Eucharist chiefly expresses '*the redemptive act of Christ the Bridegroom towards the Church the Bride*. This is clear and unambiguous when the sacramental ministry of the Eucharist, in which the priest acts "*in persona Christi*", is performed by a man.'[19] With a celibate priesthood, 'the Church itself becomes the spouse of the priest'.[20] Hence, Elizabeth Johnson states women's 'physical embodiment becomes a prison that shuts them off from God, except as mediated through a christic male'[21] and Lavinia Byrne concludes that ordaining women would be 'publicly overturning a theological order which says that biology is destiny'.[22]

Responses to Jesus' maleness from feminists who hold onto Christian tradition involve an emphasis on both the *humanity* of Jesus rather than his maleness and the liberating praxis of his life. As Mary Catherine Hilkert demonstrates, an awareness of issues pertaining to Jesus' ethnicity, social background, life experience, as well as to his maleness, indicate that questions around the person of Jesus are multi-faceted.[23] The concentration of significance on the particularity of Jesus' sex does, of course, serve a patriarchal, androcentric mind-set that seeks to affirm maleness as the human norm and consequently diminishes women both theologically and socially. Surely Elizabeth Johnson is correct when she states that Jesus' maleness is a constitutive element of his identity, part of his historical contingency, and that the difficulty arises with the way Jesus' maleness is constructed in androcentric theology and ecclesiology and that it would not 'in a more just church . . . even be an issue'.[24]

The key question remains whether women and femaleness are suitable vehicles with which to speak of the divine. Or put another way, does the fact that Jesus was male mean they are not? Pertinent to this question is the context of suffering for in such circumstances women have found comfort and strength in identifying with the suffering Jesus.[25] Such identification has produced artistic representations of women in crucified form. In 1993 Margaret Argyle, in response to the accounts of the rapes carried out on Bosnian women in the ongoing conflict in that region, crafted a four foot high work of mixed textiles she named *Bosnian Christa*[26] which portrayed a crucified female form set against a female vulva.[27] Reflecting on her completed work she said, 'This God who understands and shares such suffering speaks through a figure of a woman on a cross . . . [The cross] is about a God who is in the world and present wherever anyone suffers . . . I had never associated God with women and their suffering before.'[28]

Perceiving the image of a crucified Christ in female form is not without precedent. The martyrdom in the second century of a Christian woman called Blandina is recorded by the church historian Eusebius. He writes of her torture and her eventual death in the amphitheatre where she was, among other excessive cruelties, hung on a stake. Eusebius comments that she 'seemed to be hanging in the shape of a cross' and that the other Christians 'saw in the form of their sister him who was crucified for them'.[29]

The New Testament understanding of the church as the body of Christ endorses this correlation between Christ and women. This is most graphically illuminated in the record of the conversion experience of Paul. Following his intense and vehement persecution of Christian women and men, Paul's encounter with the risen Christ on the road to Damascus confronted him with the question, 'Why do you persecute me?' Christ's self-identification is 'I am Jesus, whom you are persecuting.' (Acts 8:3; 9:4; 9:5) Hence, Chung Hyun Kyung speaks of recognising 'the Christ disfigured in his passion' in women who have been dehumanised by oppressive systems[30] and writing of four North American Christian women murdered in El Salvador in 1980 Jon Sobrino comments that the 'murdered Christ is here in the person of four *women*'.[31] Such christological understanding endorses using femaleness in order to speak of God.

God-talk is an integral component of our understanding and experience of God. A Presbyterian woman observed that God is 'a spiritual being. I suppose, you know, we can't help have images float around in our head and I suppose God is king often. I don't think I consciously kind of think of God like that. Or mentally I think I think of God as purely spiritual, but I suppose we can't because we can't visualise what is spiritual.' The problem is not with the idea of images of God, but with their misuse. There has been and continues to be an overwhelming suppression, negation and opposition to female God-talk which is, in part, enforced by the dominant use of male images for God. Our next question, therefore, is how we may talk of the divine in ways that do justice not only to God, but also to women.

WOMEN IN GOD'S IMAGE

It is necessary for our God-talk to do justice not only to God but also to women because the way we talk of God is bound up with how we view ourselves. When one woman was asked how she thought God would describe and feel about her, she quickly responded, 'That's really asking me for what I think of myself, isn't it?'[32] Specifically, because our God-talk is this 'two-way traffic in ideas'[33] the male dominance of God-language means 'men not only model God but God, in return, bestows divine qualities on men'.[34] Hence, 'it becomes clear that this [male] exclusive speech about God serves in manifold ways to support an imaginative and structural world that excludes or subordinates women. Wittingly or not, it undermines women's human dignity as equally created in the image of God.'[35]

If our talk of God dominantly reflects male human experience and expression this inevitably affects the scope of Christian women's relationship to God and their understanding of themselves. A Catholic woman described speaking of God in exclusively male terms as like giving 'God one set of values, one set of characteristics', as if God is saying, 'I am only this here and you can only relate to me as this.' Hence, as Sallie McFague notes, 'the patriarchal model oppresses women as much by what it does *not* say about woman as by what it *does* say. What it does say defines her as inferior; what it does not say leaves her without alternatives.'[36]

It is precisely to provide an alternative that has been a significant part of the newly revived goddess movement of the last three decades. Imaging the divine as female using the language of the goddess is 'a way of exploring what it means to be a woman'.[37] While there are a variety of ways in which the term goddess is understood – as a single universal deity which is female, in terms of many goddesses, in representing divinity as a symbol of women's own self-worth, or even an understanding that combines all of these – in general, thealogy, the study of the goddess, talks in terms of the *divinity* of the female whereas Christian theology speaks of the *humanity* of women. Both are endeavouring to express women's self-worth, dignity and agency. In juxtaposition to the emphasis within patriarchal Christianity of the God-likeness of males, thealogy refers to the female as divine. A theology that seeks to be both Christian and feminist, however, focuses on the humanity of women for within a Christian framework there is no higher affirmation of personhood than speaking of humanity made in the image of God.

Christian personhood: made in the image of God

The defining aspect of a Christian view of human personhood is in the understanding of humanity made in the image of God. In biblical tradition this conviction is the basis not only for the way human beings relate to the divine, but the way that they relate to each other. The poetic narratives of Genesis chapters one and two focus on God's creating activity of the world and of human beings and are the explanatory paradigm for all that follows in biblical tradition and history. In other words, they make sense of God's dealing with humanity and the rest of creation as depicted and interpreted in the Scriptures. The New Testament emphasis on followers of Jesus being made into the image of Christ is part of the continuum of this foundational notion that humanity is made in the image of God. If humanity is made in the image of God, what are the implications for our God-talk?

Phyllis Trible states that in Genesis 1:27, which reads, 'So God created humankind in his image, in the image of God he created them; male and female he created them', the phrase 'male and female' is a metaphor for the image of God. She points out that sexual differentiation (not gender role stereotyping) is part of being made in the image of God and not simply related to procreation.[38] In addition, she argues that the phrase 'image of God' is itself a metaphor for 'God', and that this preserves the transcendence and freedom of the deity. For no matter how much God becomes understood through our metaphorical language, God is never defined by it: 'God is neither male nor female, nor a combination of the two. And yet, detecting divine transcendence in human reality requires human clues. Unique among them, according to our poem, is sexuality. God creates, in the image of God, male and female. To describe male and female, then, is to perceive the image of God; to perceive the image of God is to glimpse the transcendence of God.'[39]

The understanding of human persons as made in the image of God gives us more than a singular known reference point from which to gain insight of the divine. At minimum there are two: woman and man, let alone the enormous diversity among different peoples that each of these encompasses. It is not that there is no commonality among these metaphorical vehicles, or that the image of God can be taken to mean anything, but rather that our commonality, that is, our *humanity* made in the image of God, can be expressed in a multitude of ways and not simply in one way. There is no valid reason to continue disallowing femaleness and female experience as metaphorical vehicles for speaking of God while accepting without question metaphors from maleness and male experience. Viewing humanity as made in the image of God, existing as two sexes and with each sex expressing full human personhood, does not simply remove any barriers to God-talk from femaleness or female experience. It also requires it.

Beverley Clack comments on how God-language has an impact upon the way we understand ourselves: 'As a woman brought up in the Christian tradition, I have never heard God described in my image. I have often wondered what it would be like to hear God described habitually in female language. The difference between male and female self-esteem and self-acceptance might in part arise in response to an androcentric understanding of God. What self-confidence must come about from internalizing a message which equates one's self with God!'[40] It is just this dynamic that has been explored by Jann Aldredge Clanton. She has carried out research into the self-esteem and spirituality of women and men in relation to their God-concepts as demonstrated through language. Women whose God-concept was male consistently had lower levels of confidence, autonomy, achievement and creativity than those women whose language for God was androgynous or transcended gender.[41] Excluding females and femaleness from God-talk is a way of denying Christian women's full personhood as those who are created in the image of God. As Dorothee Sölle says in reference to patriarchy's sexist language for God, 'The concept of the natural inferiority of women and the legitimation of their subjection, which they like to present theologically as subjection given in creation, is – for both sexes, by the way – one of the greatest obstacles on the long path to becoming fully human.'[42]

A God-talk for Christian women, therefore, will restore their full personhood in their own eyes and (potentially at least for there is more at stake here than theological correctness for those opposed to the realisation of women's full personhood) in the understanding of the Christian community.

Speaking personally

The principle of using myriad ideas, both personal and impersonal, to speak of God is valuable in emphasising the enormity of the task of speaking of the divine and avoiding one particular God-concept becoming idolatrous. The value of using impersonal images is that we are not tempted to make the error of identification. In the words of Janet Morley, 'it is powerful and helpful to call God a "rock", both because God is like a rock in important ways, and because it would hardly be possible to *confuse* God with a rock. The image can be used, and then let go, which is how we should treat all religious language.'[43] However, speaking of God in personal terms is most suitable given human personhood, which is made in the image of God. Yet we must not forget that God-talk that utilises personal images remains metaphorical. Given the overwhelming dominance of male imagery used for God that influences our imagination even when gender neutral God-language is used, it is essential that female metaphors are employed to speak of God. Female God-talk is not only the best corrective to the idea that God is male. It is also the means whereby Christian women's full human personhood is restored as those who, being made in the image of God, are able to represent the divine.

Moreover, female God-talk should occur on an *habitual* basis. Occasional use merely reinforces male God-talk as normative and does little to dethrone the idol of a God who is male or the male who has 'become God'. The present situation is one in which using female God-talk is seen as an aberration. Hence, a Catholic woman in her seventies commented that, while she had read a lot about what she called 'the feminine version of

God', it was not something she employed herself: 'I have a little feeling that I could get eccentric about it so I avoid it.' The idea that female God-talk is a deviation from what is normal was spoken of by another woman. Also in her seventies she reflected, 'He can't be just a father. This is something I thought of years ago . . . but again you didn't develop these things in yourself 'cos I suppose you didn't know how . . . I mean, you would have been looked at if you'd said something like well if God made the world and God made women and men he must know as much about women as he does about men. That was something that I remember thinking years ago but where to go with that, I didn't know.'

Making female God-talk usual rather than unusual within Christian theology and experience is in part dependent on not using femaleness to represent secondary or additional rather than primary or essential aspects of the divine. However unintentional, it is possible that female God-talk could be employed in ways that only serve to reinforce the existing God – man – woman hierarchy and dualistic view of humanity. It is important to understand how this happens before looking at female God-talk that does not fall into this trap.

Female God-talk as extra

There are those who conceptualise God as having masculine and feminine characteristics. While an Anglican woman thought that God was male, she also believed there are 'what I would consider female characteristics in God. I suppose it's the same with all of us, you know, I'm female but I think I have, I can be assertive and things you associate with male characteristics. Likewise in men, I think of my husband, he's an awful lot of characteristics which would traditionally be considered to be female. So I think God is a bit like that. I suppose we talk of God being our father and that as a provider I suppose, but he's got both characteristics, I think.' Thinking of God this way often means attributing female characteristics to a male God. In the words of a Catholic woman in her sixties, 'He's male with all . . . the feminine qualities.' In this understanding, female God-talk serves to redress the imbalance of the missing so-called 'feminine' attributes of God.[44]

Others see a feminine dimension within the Trinity in the person of the Holy Spirit. 'I don't think that you can put a gender on God', said a young Catholic woman, 'the way that I see God is . . . in the image of Trinity that we have been brought up with. There's God the father, who's obviously male, God the Son – I mean there's no disputing that Jesus was a man, I don't think. And the Spirit as being the feminine . . . Now my understanding is very much of the Spirit as being the feminine.'

These ways of thinking about God, as either possessing both feminine and masculine characteristics or as having a feminine dimension, are attempts at understanding God through the lens of humanity, which is both female and male. But this lens is one which sees women and men in dualistic relationship, that is, that identifies men with certain masculine characteristics and values these over women and feminine-identified characteristics. Put another way, these views of God mirror at divine level a human patriarchal gendered division. As Rosemary Radford Ruether comments, 'In such a concept, the feminine side of God, as a secondary or mediating principle, would act in the same subordinate and limited roles in which females are allowed to act in the patriarchal social order.'[45] There is, in other words, a pecking order of gender characteristics applied to God with those that are masculine given priority and greater value over those that are feminine. This in turn serves, however unwittingly, to provide divine endorsement of a dualistic view of human gender. And, as already noted, it is this dualistic world view that itself undergirds women's subordination and the devaluing of female experience.

In addition, within this dualistic paradigm applied to God, while men may be enabled to recover their 'feminine' side, or own so-called feminine characteristics (for example, care and empathy), women are not similarly enabled to claim so-called masculine attributes (for example, power and authority) as part of their experience. If God has a feminine side, those qualities which one woman spoke of as being shaved off God when God is spoken of as male, men can take that on board. However, God does not simply have a masculine side, but is dominantly male, and women cannot appropriate this in the same way. For men, it is adding feminine characteristics to an essentially male core, for women it is identifying with the extra characteristics and not being the same as the core. It also follows that only men can represent the fullness of God, women being restricted to God's feminine characteristics. This in itself undermines the suitability of femaleness to image the divine in God-talk. The God – male – female hierarchy is endorsed and the subordination that is women's social and ecclesiastical reality is maintained.

Female God-talk as equivalence

So much for what is not meant if female God-talk is to affirm women's identity as those made in the image of God. But if it is not about feminine attributes of God, or a feminine or female dimension of God, what is it about? Female God-talk is about deity in its fullness (rather than a particular characteristic or side of the divine) being expressed in female image. In the words of Elizabeth Johnson, female God-talk involves 'the divine in images taken equivalently from the experience of women, men and the world of nature'.[46]

The female images used in this way are not simply those aspects we traditionally associate as female being used to express deity in its fullness (such as tenderness and nurture), although these do need to be included to contribute to our understanding of God. After all, each expression for the divine used in our God-talk helps in our understanding of the divine, building the picture of God which we may never say is complete. And because our talk of God has been expressed dominantly through not simply maleness but our gendered understanding of masculinity (in terms of power, might, rule and fatherly benevolence), including female God-talk can offer understanding of God which to date has been lacking. Further, the exclusion or neglect particularly of women's physicality from God-talk has impoverished our possible imaging of the divine.

However, this is not to suggest that inclusive God-talk involves restricting female or male imagery in what each can illuminate of God according to a (stereotypically) dualistic gendered understanding of humanity. God, who is not of human sex or gender but the creator of female and male, can be represented, for example, as compassionate and powerful in both male and female images. Hence, to use biblical imagery, the God who redeems lost humanity is portrayed in male imagery of shepherd and father *and* in female image of a householder/ homemaker. The God who acts powerfully on behalf of God's own people is portrayed by male images of hero and man of war *and* the female image of a woman in labour (see Luke 15; Isaiah 42:13 – 14). These are equivalent images. Inclusive imaging of God is needed, for without female God-talk used to express the fullness and variety of the divine, male God-talk risks becoming idolatrous. It is the presence of male *and* female God-talk that means the metaphorical nature of all personal images may be retained. It is the inclusion of female God-talk that contributes to restoring Christian women's full personhood in the acknowledgement of their suitability to image the divine.

To grasp speaking of God in inclusive images of equivalence is as much to confront the underlying dualism that is part of the very fabric of our thinking about women and men as it is to challenge our ideas about God. In other words, in using female imagery for God we do not simply identify those things with which women are perhaps most comfortable and equate these with the divine in female form. Janet Morley comments that despite her liturgical use of female God-talk, when confronted with a friend in shocking pain dying of cancer she found herself raging against God because of the suffering her friend was experiencing. She realised that in this context God was 'him':

'Somehow it was easier to fight a God I could associate with the forces of patriarchy; how much more disturbing to confront "her". But it really will not do for me to call God "she" only when I mean what is tender and unproblematic; this is a new kind of dualism. If I do this, I am identifying God's difficult "otherness" with the otherness that I experience in relation to masculinity . . . [This] is a false parallel. It is the wrong kind of "otherness".'[47]

This demonstrates the pervasiveness of the dualistic framework in how we think. By attributing to God who is she only that which is 'warm, attractive and motherly'[48] the dualistic paradigm remains intact both theologically and in human relations. There is an otherness in respect of God that relates to transcendence, but not to the alienation involved in dualism. Jann Aldredge Clanton says that for men who always envisage God as male, otherness is not something they experience: 'For their own spiritual wholeness, men need images of God beyond the masculine. When all references to God are masculine, men cannot feel as deeply as women the Otherness of God.'[49]

Generally, the issues in regard to our understanding of God are different for women and men. For women it is their alienation from self-identification with God and subsequent social subordination in contrast to men's over-identification with the divine and social dominance. However, what is needed for both is a breaking out of a dualistic paradigm and affirming that God is neither male nor female but may (and indeed in this context must) be known through a multiplicity of human experiences which must be gender inclusive to avoid a false identification of deity with maleness and a negation of women's full personhood. This gender inclusion is not in terms of traditional dualistic assignations of males and females, but involves the endeavours of men and women *in being human*.

It is not that talk of God becomes only talk of ourselves. Daphne Hampson has commented how in much feminist theology talk of God has been replaced by talk of women's experience, not even women's experience of God.[50] However, understanding God through human experience in all its commonality and particularity is to explicate the notion of humanity made in God's image. Such unpacking involves opening up the horizon of God-talk to include a wealth of human experience and invite the kind of imagining which has not previously been encouraged or allowed. Human experience in this sense is as wide ranging as, for example, our social situatedness, the fact that we are embodied persons, our particular physicality, and our relationships with others and the world. All are ways of trying to give articulation to our understanding of God that does justice both to women (and men) and the divine.

In all of this the need is for God-talk that affirms Christian women's personhood as made in the image of God, providing the theological framework for ending the violation of personhood of which women's subordination consists.

Chapter 3

HIS AND HER GOSPELS:
Inequality, gender and identity

I don't like thinking about being myself and what I am . . . I try to think of others . . . My understanding of Christianity is that I'm here to serve, I'm not here to make more of myself or less of myself, I'm here to serve and be faithful.

Presbyterian woman in her forties

I would immediately feel . . . the needs of other people are more important than the needs of you, which would be my way of thinking. Is that because of my low self-esteem again, I don't know? . . . It teaches in the Bible that you put others before yourself.

Presbyterian woman under forty

I think my faith probably was the biggest drawback because the only thing I remember being taught was that I should live for others . . . Nobody ever taught me to love myself.

Catholic woman in her fifties

Our sense of personal identity, whether we are able to articulate it or not, is crucial to our life experience. How we view ourselves, what we believe about ourselves, and our sense of the extent of our own worth, is fundamental to our personal development and social existence. All of this is affected by our culture, our relationships, our social reality, for feminists, our feminist vision and, for Christians, our faith.

The Christian idea of humanity made in the image of God invests intrinsic worth and value in human persons. This is what a Protestant woman is reflecting when she says, 'I see myself as someone that God has made and therefore with a place in the world and with importance in the whole scheme of things.' However, for Christian women this inherent worth can be contradicted by the interaction of three dynamics. These are structural inequalities, a social construction of gender which subordinates women, and a particular understanding of Christian self-denial. Basically, society is organised in a way that relies on women taking care of other people (and particularly men) while at the same time disvaluing (negating or removing value from) what they do. This arrangement is sustained by the belief that this situation is natural for women, or the way God made them. So in this context the idea of self-denial, which is very much a part of the Christian gospel, takes on a very different meaning for women than it does for men. As with the way we speak of God, our theological understanding and social relations are interwoven, in this instance to the detriment of women.

BUILT-IN INEQUALITY

'It annoys me, being a woman', said a mother in her forties, 'that your time isn't valued . . . when you're this sort of full-time at home woman that I am. I don't say I'm not working because I do work, but I'm not paid and I'm not terribly acknowledged and sometimes I feel taken for granted as a woman.' She went on to give examples of the kind of assumptions that people made about her as a woman: 'If [my husband] goes to leave the car in they press another car on him, oh you'll need a car because you've got a suit and a tie, you obviously are somebody important, you need to go somewhere important, so you get a car. Whereas maybe that day he is only going to the office and then going back to pick the car up again. Whereas, you know, because I'm in a track suit and have got grey hair and look mumsy, I'm not important. So I have to say, please can I have a car because one of my roles is taxi-ing . . . I've got to be in three different places this afternoon at a certain time. But you've got to make a big point of it and you've got to book a week in advance if you want a courtesy car. That's the last situation where I thought I wish I had a suit and tie on and I would get the respect here. I think it's a pity that. Also they assume, you know, if they say they'll call at the house at half nine it doesn't really matter if they're not there till half ten 'cos she's hanging around that place anyway – her time does not matter. That's what frustrates me about being a woman.'

What this woman is talking about is the lack of value placed on herself as a carer of her household, which she does 'full-time', in contrast to the esteem that her husband is afforded as someone employed in the workforce. She is experiencing first hand the consequences of social arrangements that divide the world into public and private domains, in which issues of care are viewed as belonging to the private arena, which itself is considered the responsibility of women. This division (or dichotomy) between the public world of work, economics and politics, and the private world of domesticity and familial concerns is another example of a dualistic framework that not only divides responsibilities into two spheres, but views them in opposition, giving one higher value than the other. In its gendered form, the assumption is that 'women are somehow "naturally" fitted for the private sphere and men for the public because each sex "naturally" possesses the moral and cognitive capacities best suited to each domain'.[1] So, men's self-identity is asserted in the public sphere ordered by concepts of rights-based justice and abstract reason. Women's assumed role is to provide service in the private realm, which involves emotional attachment, rather than the emotionally distanced objectivity required in the public world. This service, however, is undervalued precisely because it concerns the private world where women, according to the dualistic system, belong. What we have is society structured in a way that both reflects and perpetuates the disvaluing (and hence disadvantage) of women's concerns and responsibilities (which actually are human concerns and responsibilities).

The disvaluing of women's responsibilities as wives and mothers and those who maintain the home is sometimes internalised by women themselves. So while a Protestant woman spoke of how she 'always wanted to be a wife and a mother and that's what I am role-wise', she went on to say, 'I find it a wee bit difficult at times, you know. Everybody seems to work and have a job and a career and I try not to get into that comparing myself with other people because you feel a bit, you know, what is this, does this count? And I need to reinforce that it does count.' A Methodist woman echoed similar struggles: 'I wouldn't like to be thought of as a wee woman, you know . . . domesticated, constantly talking about her husband and family and that's her life. I wouldn't like to be thought of in that respect, although I can talk about those things as a woman . . . but I would like to think that I'm more interesting than that . . . There's more to life than that . . . My husband and my family mean everything to me but, you know, I have a life too and I have to have something for myself as well.' This woman is reflecting the difficulty women have in loving their families *and* pursuing interests outside of those relationships, given that these two are put in contradiction in society. In wanting to pursue her own interests outside of domestic responsibilities for her own sake, she mirrors back (albeit unintentionally) society's assessment of those who care in the private sphere, which belittles them ('a wee woman') and finds them of little interest.

The inequality inherent in the responsibilities women carry in regard to their families[2] was passionately articulated by one woman: 'I think the liberal feminists are right when it comes to single women. I think if you're a single, articulate, educated, middle-class woman you can probably fight the men fairly well on their own battleground. You can make choices, you can beat them at their own game. I didn't feel discriminated against as a woman until I became a mother. Now because until then I had my Ph.D., that was a weapon and I used it as such . . . I was able to beat them at their own game because I was better than them. So . . . until that point I . . . could compete with anyone. Then I got married, well that messed things up because my choices were constrained, but still it didn't mess it up that much. Then I had children. Now for me at that point my world collapsed and I mean having children was the most major blow ever in my life . . . Having children put me on a par with everybody else. It totally disempowered me. It robbed me of everything that made me equal and I was stuck with these screaming little brats, who were absolutely wonderful . . . [but] I was prevented from managing my time.' She described how she had given up her career to care for her children, tried to be a perfect mother, and how she had internalised everybody's expectations and, hence, the guilt she felt at not producing the perfect family: 'All the time you're fighting against the perception that because you're a mother you're letting everybody down.' While she did not regret motherhood and emphasised that it was not that she did not love her children, she had found being a mother 'the most painful thing on earth' because it had made her powerless and drained her of her energies: 'It's just the sense of no control, lack of control, control of time.' She therefore experienced so much of what she did as a struggle for which she tended to blame herself: 'I think I am left with the feeling that I am very difficult. Now I'm not actually sure that I'm that difficult, but I think that in order to get anything I've had to fight . . . The only way I can get out of situations of powerlessness is to throw a tantrum and part of me says this is you being difficult and part of me says I have to fight this so much that I go over the top . . . but I feel it's the only way I'm heard. And then you've got that guilt about making a fuss because women aren't supposed to make a fuss. So I really do think . . . it's about taking power. It's not about disempowering men but it's such a . . . fight and then you are just seen as difficult and stroppy.'

This woman is very aware not only of the powerlessness that results from the responsibility of caring in the face of unrealistic expectations from other people. She also knows the psychological harm to the self that can occur through both the lack of support she experienced and trying to challenge this. She feels she is being difficult and that others will think this. For women 'are bound internally and externally by obligations to care without complaints, on pain of becoming a bad woman: unfeminine, ungenerous, uncaring'.[3] However, as Jean Baker Miller points out, women acting out of their assigned social role are not creating conflict, rather 'they are exposing the fact that conflict exists'.[4] While women handle the conflict by remaining uncomplaining in their social roles, the conflict remains hidden and the public/private dichotomy unchallenged. And women are more likely to remain uncomplaining in their social roles if to break out of these is to face the accusation of being unwomanly, that is, to have their female identity questioned. In this we see the second dynamic that operates to undermine women's sense of their own worth. For femininity, understood in such gendered terms, in opposition to masculinity, is a social construction that serves to maintain women's subordination.

IT'S HER NATURE?

The gendered dualistic framework that constructs a God – man – woman hierarchy (discussed in chapters one and two) also finds expression in a construction of masculinity and femininity which assigns particular human characteristics along gendered lines. So, those things associated with care and nurture, like sensitivity, emotion and service, are considered feminine and those things modelled on independence, such as rationality, leadership and justice, are considered masculine. These divisions are considered natural, part of the created order and as such are given divine endorsement. Such a gender hierarchy, however, inhibits personhood for both women and men and in particular fosters women's inequality.

In its worst form, a socially constructed gender hierarchy hosts the idea of women's weakness of character (itself a value assessment of so-called feminine characteristics), which is reflected in their being given the onus of responsibility for humanity's alienation from God. (The roots of this view originate in a dualism that identifies women as material and sensual as opposed to men as spiritual and rational. Women are thus seen as the source of sexual temptation, which threatens men's spirituality.) As a Catholic woman in her sixties explained, 'I was taught it was a sin to love yourself because, you know, you were a woman, and deceitful and second Eves and all of those things.' A more common understanding of gender relations today, which claims to reject women's subordination, is of men and women as equal but complementary. As a Presbyterian woman over fifty said, 'I can't pinpoint it, but I do think [men and women] are very different in the whole way in which we think and feel and perceive. And I think that's to do as much with who we are as to our environment and what we imbibe about who we are.' A Catholic woman in her thirties agrees: 'I certainly think I would have different sensitivities to a man . . . and we talk differently and I think as women we think differently and have different ways around things.' This view of gender complementarity chooses to emphasise the difference between women and men but, as Jane Shaw points out, 'operates in such a way that women and men are seen as different but *unequal*'.[5] This was perceived by a Catholic woman who commented about men's attitude to women: 'A lot of them don't see them as equals at all, and in most relationships they don't see them as equals, even [if] they pretend they do at the back of it all, they don't. In most situations they don't treat women well. I don't mean they're brutal or physically abusing them, they just don't see them as equal . . . they won't give them a chance. There's a role for women in the world and they keep them there.'

The problem for women (and men) is that the view of sex complementarity defines what it means to be a woman or man according to stereotypes. So, because women are seen essentially as child-bearers and rearers, they are often eulogised for their gentle natures and caring abilities. They are followers not leaders. A Methodist woman in her fifties put this somewhat starkly when she explained, 'I have this idea that the man takes the decisions if . . . there is to be a deciding vote . . . If there were a deciding vote it is agreed that my husband would take it. I was given the option at marriage to say obey or not and my husband said he wouldn't marry me if I didn't say I'd obey, but I was going to anyway.'

Characteristic of complementarianism is the idea of women as complementary help to men. This is reflected, for example, in the idea that the principle of help is ontological to women, that is, is intrinsic to their being.[6] As Daphne Hampson comments, 'A good way of marking the male concept of "complementarity" is to note that the female is always to "complement" the male and never *vice versa*. That is to say, he is subject, while she is "the other".'[7]

In the view of gender complementarity, women's place is clearly defined and so long as women remain within this place they are accepted and praised, any deviation is considered to make a woman unfeminine, or even dangerous and a threat to family stability. So, for example, James Dobson, founder of *Focus on the Family* (an American religious organisation dedicated to preserving traditional values and the institution of the family), described the 1995 UN World Conference on Women held in Beijing with over 40,000 delegates as 'the greatest threat to the family in my life-time'.[8]

In such a context there can be a pressure to conform in order to be accepted. Speaking of her growing awareness that she was projecting an image, her behaviour 'always being consistent of being a girly girl', a young Protestant woman reflected: 'An awful lot of my attitudes and the way I react and the things I do, before I do them, it clicks into the fact that I'm a girl and I'm supposed to necessarily have that image of reacting that sort of way because of being a girl . . . Over the past number of years I have always reacted the way I was expected to . . . I'm thinking specifically I suppose . . . with my boyfriend. He's always looked at me as, outwardly anyway, as a girl, as feminine . . . naive, or not liking crude talk, things like that, not liking to do certain things. And now I'm thinking I don't want to be like that anymore. I want to actually say whatever I feel and irrespective of the backdrop, it's not necessarily very feminine, it's not necessarily what a girl should see or what a girl should say.'

For women who do not fit into gendered norms the frustrations they experience are very real. A Protestant woman in her fifties recalled how as a child, 'I just enjoyed the really active rough and tumble things. [And at church] I would rather be in there doing things, discussing things, making decisions, with men rather than sitting being told what to do . . . There are certain aspects to being a woman that I had to work at and still don't sit comfortably on my shoulders. I mean, I still love climbing trees!' A Catholic woman also in her fifties made a similar point: 'Some of the things I wanted to do in my life were predominately male things that men only do. For instance, studying theology, thinking about theology, talking about theology is just something that men do. I didn't do it for a long time . . . [and] a lot of people didn't understand why I was doing it.' That climbing trees, taking an active participation in the life of a local congregation, and studying theology are considered appropriate only for men is not about how women and men are created in the image of God. It is about how our gender identity has been and continues to be constructed by social forces and human decisions.

This does not mean that female human embodiment has nothing to do with female identity formation. Nor does it mean that so-called feminine qualities are not valuable in and of themselves. For example, to attune and attend to the needs of others is a vital component of human existence for all concerned. However, it is the context in which these characteristics operate that is in question, that is, one which assigns these aspects of human personhood to a subordinate position of lesser value. In other words, while aspects of being human are divided according to a hierarchical gender system, then those aspects which are associated with femaleness will be undervalued. This hierarchical, dualistic, gendered understanding of humanity impoverishes both women and men in that it inhibits their personal development as human beings. For women in particular, however, this impoverishment involves their subordination as they carry the responsibilities of the private world in a context that undervalues ideologically and practically their concerns. What is more, this situation is further endorsed by its mixing in a particular way with the Christian notion of self-denial.

CHRISTIAN IDENTITY AND DENIAL OF THE SELF

Within a Christian framework the value of persons is affirmed in the understanding that we are lovingly created in the image of God. However, for Christian women, their personhood can be undermined or violated by a particular application of a Christian understanding of self-denial, self-sacrifice and service of the self to others. The question at issue is whether a Christian identity which advocates self-giving can support women's full humanity given their social and political (and, indeed, as considered in chapter five, ecclesiastical) subordination. In other words, is a Christian identity of self-worth based on self-denial not self-defeating for Christian women in their current reality of structural inequality and hierarchical gender socialisation?

Self-denial has been a defining feature of Christian identity within Christian tradition. It derives not only from the explicit words of Jesus that to follow him people would need to deny themselves and take up their cross (see Mark 8:34), but also from the life of Jesus as one who came to serve others and his death understood as sacrifice for others (Mark 10:45). Further, such self-denial is seen as the essence of love towards others, often referred to as *agape*, 'that love which does not count the cost, which, without regard for self, thinks only of another'.[9] The important point within this traditional understanding of self-denial is that the service of others comes at the *expense* of the self. The choice is presented as between self and other. The traditional Christian response to this option is to choose the other and to deny the self. In the words of a Presbyterian woman, 'I try to be selfless in the way I live my life, I suppose that's the only way you could describe it . . . but that wouldn't have been my nature before I knew the Lord.' The same idea is framed negatively by another woman: 'I'm a bit self-willed, which can be the biggest drawback in trying to serve God.' Speaking of her entry into religious life in the Catholic church one woman explained, 'You were supposed to die to yourself. In fact when you made your profession you lay on the floor and this black rug was placed over you and there was five minutes of chanting . . . and you were now dead to the world.'

In the understanding of human relationships which subordinates women to men and which associates care and nurture with femaleness, self-denial itself finds a gendered expression within Christianity. Service of others is seen as women's particular vocation. So, while self-denial is part of Christian identity for men, this is normally applied within the parameters of a socially constructed masculinity. Therefore, it produces different consequences than does self-denial for women. In other words, self-denial for men does not disturb a hierarchical social and theological order which subordinates women in the reality of inequality and gender socialisation. Self-denial for men does not mean they give up their position of power over women. In fact, women's self-denial serves to endorse male privilege.

Theological expressions of a gendered application of self-denial are at times explicit as in the statement about 'those ordinary women who reveal the gift of their womanhood by placing themselves at the service of others in their everyday lives. For in giving themselves to others each day, women fulfil their deepest vocation.'[10] Hence, 'women have too often found in practice that Christian self-sacrifice means the sacrifice of women for the sake of men'.[11] As a Catholic woman in her fifties commented, the message that had been drummed into her before she was five years old was that her purpose in life was to help men. She talked about 'the sacrificial element of the female, sacrifice yourself for the male'.

This powerful combination of self-denial, self-sacrifice, self-spent in the service of others, operated within a dualistic framework in which 'men have espoused an ethic which they did not practise; [and] women have practised it to their detriment',[12] produces an unhealthy view of women by themselves and others. This denies women's full human personhood, inherent to which is a notion of their own intrinsic value and worth. In contrast to the growing sense of their own worth expressed by some women (see below), there were those whose talk of themselves revolved around a sense of unworthiness, of failure, guilt, and of being nothing special. A Presbyterian woman in her forties said this of herself: 'I would have a poor self-image. I probably would put myself down . . . In most aspects of my life I would feel there's other people more capable . . . and I'm very happy to be second fiddle.' She talked about how she worried what people would think of God because of her, and she began to cry. She reflected further: 'I think I've been discouraged down through years of going to church, being preached at, you should be this, you should be that . . . instead of being encouraged. I think that's my church experience . . . You're constantly being assessed aren't you? Your parents assess you, you're assessed at school, you're constantly being assessed . . . and spiritually in a way then you're being assessed too.'

This sense of being assessed by religious 'authorities' was also expressed by a Catholic woman in her forties. Commenting on her life she realised, 'I was far too judgemental on myself and I was too hard on me and I think that was because every time, no matter what I did, there was always a judgement made on it.' Another example of a lack of self-valuing came from a woman in her fifties who had a complete sense of her own inferiority, with *nothing* good to say of herself: 'Oh help. [I see myself] as very insignificant. As inadequate. As not very good at anything. As inferior, [inferior to] other women. I don't think I'm very good at anything.' There was no sense of distress as she described herself this way, she even laughed as she went through a list of her own inadequacies. For her, her faith had helped her to accept her self-assessed inferiority: 'I said my view of myself is that I'm inferior but I don't feel inferior. I feel that I am where God wants me to be and he is with me and he has made me, therefore I am content with that. It's OK, yes, that's the way I'm made.' She assigns herself a God-given subordinate position: she is inferior. Her discomfort with her own identity was hinted at near the beginning of the interview when after responding to several questions she commented: 'This is all "I" isn't it? . . . It doesn't seem right to be talking about myself all the time.'

Citing these examples of women's experience is not to suggest that such difficult religious experience is the prerogative of women any more than it is to suggest there are no issues around Christian self-denial and the construction of masculinity. However, this negative religious experience contributes in a particular way to women's self-negation, disvaluing and diminishment given its interplay with cultural dynamics. It is also not the case that such self-negation is only the experience of Christian women. As Jean Baker Miller notes, 'Women are taught that their main goal in life is to serve others — first men, and later, children.'[13] However, the theological tradition of self-denial with its gendered expression that is part of a context of inequality and socially constructed femininity, provides divine imperative for women's neglect of themselves, exacerbating their situation and robbing them of aspects of their own personhood. As Carter Heyward remarks, 'To relinquish our moral agency and the critical necessity of becoming self-affirming, self-respecting people who can assume responsibility for shaping our lives in the world is to give up the purposefulness and creative power of being human in God's world.'[14]

Matters of self and other, so much a part of the Christian gospel that concerns not only how we respond to God but how we relate to each other, go to the heart of our identity and cannot be easily dismissed, even though they are frequently unexplored. Yet, even as we begin to open up the subject, we find ourselves confronted with a major obstacle. Namely that the paradigm in which the discussion occurs is itself problematic. In other words, the choice presented between self and other is a false choice; there is an alternative way of viewing this relationship which values both self and other. This is one that puts humans in an alternative paradigm that views us in a relational rather than oppositional mode. As we shall now explore, this changes the nature of the conversation about self and other in a way that fosters rather than hinders women's personal identity as those made in the image of God.

YOU SHALL LOVE YOURSELF AS YOUR NEIGHBOUR

'You shall love your neighbour as yourself', said Jesus (Luke 10:27). It may seem obvious, but if you are to love your neighbour as yourself then you must love yourself! Yet rarely is that notion given consideration when thinking about these words of Jesus. It is as if we stop reading after the phrase 'love your neighbour', concentrating all meaning and relevance in that phrase, and forget that 'as yourself' follows. So influential has been the gendered tradition of self-denial that thinking about loving both ourselves *and* our neighbours appears an absent concept, let alone the idea that the two are integrally related! The reason for reversing their order in the above heading is to draw attention to just this – sometimes we need to say things a little differently in order to hear what is actually being said. The presumption of love of self in what Jesus said has got lost in women's subordinated reality.

It is central to feminist thinking that in order to value both the self and others, rather than seeing them as set in contradiction, the self must be understood in *relation* to others rather than in *opposition* to them. In contrast, therefore, to speaking of an individual self who finds their definition in separation from others, feminists speak of a 'self-in-relations',[15] or a self 'centred in relation'.[16] This language acknowledges that identities are formed through interaction with others and, what is more, it values these connections. This view contrasts with a masculinist framework for understanding the self which values the self as an autonomous individual who needs to separate from others in order to develop an emotional distancing that is required as a protective barrier to self-assertive rights-claims. It is not that the feminist concept of the relational self disregards the importance of autonomy. But it is an autonomy that develops in context, amid connections, and with emotional expressivity.

While these two understandings of the self – as relational and separated – are gender related, this is not to suggest that they are biologically determined, that is, that women and men inevitably develop this way. Rather, as we shall see, relational and separated identities may be attributed to social construction. It is also not the case that the experience of women in the present context is necessarily preferred. For in the current situation of the expectation and reliance upon women to care for others, a sense of connection to others without an accompanying sense of their own selves can be to women's detriment. The path to valuing self and other is not as even or as straightforward as we might like it to be!

Self-in-relation

The orientation towards others that is so much a part of women's experience was encapsulated by Jean Baker Miller writing in 1976: 'If we look at what women have been doing in life, we see that a large part of it can be called "active participation in the development of others".'[17] As a Catholic woman put it, 'I care about others and I try to help other people.' For a Presbyterian woman, contributing to the well-being of others was central to her identity: 'I like to think that I'm a caring person, and a helpful person and a person who works . . . for the good of others really. I'd like people to see the beauty of Jesus in my life, I hope people do, that's something I would want . . . I enjoy helping other people.' In describing herself as 'someone who wanted to do something good in the community' an Anglican woman is also reflecting this orientation of women to care for others.

When talking about why it is that women believe in God more than men do, those interviewed included the idea that this was because of women's caring role/nature, their experience as mothers and/or their sociability. They also related women's belief in God to women's acknowledgement of their own need, their dependence or sense of vulnerability in contrast to men's independence and self-sufficiency. Regardless of the truth or otherwise of the women's observations about belief in God, what is relevant here is that women identify the characteristics of care and need of connection as part of women's experience and contrast this to men's.[18]

This orientation of women to the well-being of others has

been attributed to their early developmental experience of being in connection with others, specifically their mothers. Nancy Chodorow argues that given that the primary care of the young is largely carried out by mothers (or other women), children in traditional families form their identities in relation to their mothers, this typically being a different experience for girls than for boys. A girl's sense of her own identity need not be achieved in contrast to her mother whom she identifies as being like herself. For a boy, however, the task of differentiation and individuation wherein he forms his own personality is done not simply in contrast to but in opposition to his mother, to the extent of making her an object against which he grows. Hence, 'girls come to define and experience themselves as continuous with others; their experience of self contains more flexible or permeable ego boundaries. Boys come to define themselves as more separate and distinct, with a great sense of rigid ego boundaries and differentiation. The basic feminine sense of self is connected to the world, the basic masculine sense of self is separate.'[19]

Further, Nancy Chodorow suggested that boys' development in opposition to their mothers results in boys learning to put down everything they associate as feminine.[20] This lesson learned young is carried into adulthood and finds expression in the disvaluing of so-called feminine characteristics, which simply endorses women's subordinated position. Therefore, as Daphne Hampson notes, the male adulation of the feminine in the view of sex complementarity is not a veneration of actual women who 'have commonly been despised, their most elementary rights flouted'.[21]

That women's identity is profoundly connected to their relationships to others was demonstrated in the research of Carol Gilligan. Her work began as a challenge to existing psychological theories in which women's development was often viewed as immature because it did not complete the established stages of moral development. In her research Carol Gilligan discerned what she described as 'a different voice' among women in which their sense of connection with others influenced their identity and morality.[22] The contrast is between 'a self defined through separation and a self delineated through connection, between a self measured against an abstract ideal of perfection and a self assessed through particular activities of care'.[23] She conceptualised men's way of structuring relationships in terms of hierarchy and women's in terms of a web.

With service to others involving denial of the self it is the masculinist model that dominates. Indeed, Daphne Hampson argues that it is this sense of separation and disconnection that has been used to create the Western Christian tradition's view of a God who is remote, unconnected and distant from humanity.[24] However, the idea of relationality being intrinsic to the nature of God is also evident within Christian tradition.

It exists in the concept of God as Trinity, which enshrines the idea of 'personhood, being-in-relation-to-another' as 'the ultimate originating principle of all reality'.[25] In the gospel accounts, Jesus speaks of relationality as both foundational and integral to humanity's encounter with God. The commandment to love God with all heart, soul, mind and strength is linked to the commandment to love your neighbour as you love yourself.[26] These two commandments are described as the greatest commandments, which encapsulate all the teaching of the law and the prophets, in other words, the existing religious tradition. They place relationship at the heart of all human activity and life and experience of God. Relationship to God and relationship to others are inseparably linked here. Further, love of others is placed on a mutual footing with love of self so that 'love is not to deny I am a valuable and irreplaceable individual, it is to acknowledge that you are too'.[27] This relation between love of God, self and others is endorsed by the 'new commandment' of Jesus that his followers should love others as they have been loved by himself, and in the 'golden rule' to do to others as you would have them do to you.[28] The radical nature of the latter is seen when read against an existing but negative form of this saying in the ancient world, not to do to others what you would not want done to yourself.

In all of these things there is a correct valuing and respecting of the self and others as those whom God loves. 'My belief is that I have to be reconciled to myself, my neighbour, or through myself and my neighbour to God', said a Catholic woman in her thirties. 'And that I can't say that I love God – you can't love God, and have a relationship with God and not be in a relationship with people, it doesn't work, you know. It has to be in union, you know, and part of that is to be reconciled with yourself.' For an Anglican woman in her forties her faith was 'not so much an individual thing between me and God but . . . a communal thing. To me I think it's about God and his people. And I have experienced quite deep senses of belonging in different churches . . . and probably acceptance from other people has in turn, you know, made real God's acceptance of me.'

It is this understanding of the relationship between love of God, neighbour and self that too often has been absent in Christian experience, and the import of self-love and acceptance for Christian spirituality neglected. This is lucidly articulated by a Catholic woman: 'I think my faith probably was the biggest drawback because the only thing I remember being taught was that I should live for others. Now I learnt a rhyme as a child and it was, "Others, yes Lord, others, let this my motto be, grace to live for others that I may live for thee". Nobody ever taught me to live for me, *ever*. And . . . I mean it doesn't work. Christ's idea of loving other people is fine, but he said love others as you love yourself. Nobody ever taught me to love myself. Consequently I probably would have died on my feet, which I nearly did. I did not know how to look after myself, it has taken a long time to learn . . . My faith did not teach me to look after myself.'

It is against the background of a Christian imperative to deny the self along with the strong gendered assumption that women will do so, that many women neglect their own needs and desires and find themselves exploited and diminished. So, for these women, their sense of connection and identification with others needs to be partnered with a sense of their own autonomy.

Self-in-relation

Many women get uncomfortable when talking about themselves. 'Really, honestly', explained a Catholic woman in her seventies, 'I don't like talking about myself. I would sometimes get embarrassed. I think it's been inbred to us, you don't talk about yourself.' An Anglican woman in her forties said of the experience, 'This is very difficult because you don't want to give yourself compliments.'

This tendency to presume that self-consideration is a negative characteristic is reflected by women who spoke about thinking of themselves in terms of selfishness or self-centredness. So in contrast to her putting 'other people's needs first – to be honest maybe to the point of [it] being a problem', an Anglican woman under forty spoke of 'learning to reason what's important and what's not' yet added, 'I find it hard to be more self-centred.' Another woman who tended 'to go a bit overboard on other people's needs', describing herself as having 'a problem with that' commented, 'I would have to be careful about that and remind myself about my own needs and not to feel that that's selfish.'

Given the dis-ease around women focusing on themselves, when speaking of women's personal development, enhancement, self-awareness or autonomy, we should bear in mind that we do so in a context where women generally have not had such self-valuing. Daphne Hampson explains: 'What men (and non-feminist women) need to grasp is that in constructing a discourse about assertiveness, rights and autonomy, women are starting from a different place from that which privileged men have occupied. Self-deprecation is still the lot of most women, including women who to all appearances have outwardly achieved in a "male" world. It is within such a context that women's talk of empowerment should be understood. It should not be confused with "power over" or exploitation of others.'[29]

It is also necessary to keep in mind what is being proposed. We are not talking about an autonomy that cuts women off from others because it views independence as more valuable and advantageous. Rather, in speaking of women's coming into their own or self-realisation, 'one is speaking of coming to oneself-in-relationship; able, through having come into one's own, to be present in a new way to others'.[30] Put simply by a Catholic woman: 'We do need our self-images – if you're kind to yourself you'll be kind to others.'

Robin Dillon states that '[f]ew things are as important to our well-being as a secure sense of our own worth, or as debilitating and disempowering as its lack'.[31] She argues that self-understanding is a necessary condition for self-respect[32] for in taking ourselves seriously, responding to ourselves as knowers, and seeing ourselves as those who need to be understood, we are expressing the value we place on ourselves.[33] Robin Dillon maintains that self-neglect is incompatible with self-respect.[34] By self-neglect she means not only outward disregard for our appearance, which is easily acknowledged as a sign of lost self-respect, but the deeper forms of self-neglect, 'ignoring one's needs, intuitions, emotional nature, and so on, as women are traditionally encouraged to do'.[35] She suggests that the first step to self-respect is to pay the right attention to oneself.[36]

The journey on this road to self-discovery was illustrated by a Catholic woman in her seventies who had 'spent most of my life doing things for other people or taking [care of] my mother first of all, and then when I got married my husband – and what he said went – and then your children'. While she stated she was not unhappy about this she referred to an incident concerning her children that occurred when she was in her forties: 'My husband said, well as a mother you should have done this, you should have done that and, something just snapped [*snapped her fingers*] and I said, "But am I just a mother, am I just a wife, am I just a daughter? Where's me, you know, where's me?" and "I'm not a me". I mean, that was said sort of in anger, you know, but after that I suppose I began to think about it, yes I am a me. Although I'm in a situation where I have to do [many things], at the same time I can be myself and have my own thoughts and I don't have to think the way other people think. So that was the beginning of any introspection or looking into myself.'

Trudy Govier has linked self-respect to self-trust for self-trust is necessary for a person to be able to think and decide for themselves and so function as an autonomous human being. 'Only with self-trust can one conduct one's own life so as to lead an authentic personal existence not open to domination by other people, social convention, or passing fads.'[37] One woman expressed how her faith had clearly enhanced her own self-belief and ability to act on this: 'I feel that at times God has led me to do things that are not conformist and yet I have felt it was right and then it was confirmed it was right . . . I think assurance of God's love to me sort of gives you the courage to trust yourself and gives you freedom to go and do things that . . . people would find a bit risky, you know, or against what my family would have [thought].'

The potential of this self-trust to cause women to act independently with integrity can be hampered by their orientation to relationships with others. Carol Gilligan[38] concluded from her research that many women have problems with differentiation of the self. As a result of women's orientation to connection they fear disconnection, while men with a separated identity fear attachment. Speaking of her lack of assertiveness in situations which required her to confront issues with other people, a Protestant woman in her fifties commented, 'I suppose it boils down to not wanting to offend people, I suppose it's as basic as that. I will do it when I really have to, but it takes a lot out of me.' A Presbyterian woman in her forties encapsulated the implications of hurting others: 'I'm probably too much influenced by other people's feelings. I would find it very hard to hurt people, probably bend over backwards to please them in this kind of silly nonsense at times when you'd be far better to be firm and stick by things . . . I think for somebody like me who finds it very hard to hurt people's feelings, it's very difficult to balance things . . . You don't want to hurt their feelings in case they won't like you so well.' The key phrase here is her concern that *'they won't like you so well'*. While attention to the opinions of others is part of social existence, it can be problematic if it causes women (or anyone) to act against their own integrity and in ways that they know are to their detriment.

Many women spoke of themselves in ways that were warm and generous as well as honest. And many had found their faith (if not always their religious heritage) constructive in their personal development, which was very much 'work in progress'. Frequently women spoke of coming to accept, respect and trust themselves as an ongoing process. In particular, among many of the women there was a sense of burden, struggle and pain associated with their own self-understanding and working that out in the context of their responsibilities and relationships to others, which were deeply ingrained as their primary responsibility before thinking of themselves. The difficulty women have in being true to their identities as selves-in-relation, that is in valuing both themselves and others, is expressed when they address the conflict they experience when their own needs compete with the needs of others.

Negotiating between self and other

To affirm the reality and value of ourselves as social beings is not to suggest that our relationships are not subject to conflicting needs between ourselves and others. It is in the tension inherent in this conflict of needs that women struggle with their sense of themselves, their responsibilities to others, their spiritual integrity and their religious traditions.

Dealing with competing needs is part of the fabric of daily life. Women view this dilemma in different ways. For some, their Christian understanding was that the needs of others should take priority. 'I think in those situations I always feel that the thing that I should do as a Christian' said a young Protestant woman, 'and the thing that God would want me to do, you know, if Jesus was here what he would do, you know, would always be to sacrifice what I wanted and what I need for the other person.'

Other women, while holding to this Christian understanding of putting others first, were also trying to negotiate care of themselves. For a Presbyterian woman in her forties: 'My faith challenges me to carry one another's burdens and to think of others first and to be a cheerful giver. I suppose I've always had the perception of what's demanded of me is that I think of others first or whatever. But having said [that], I do also feel learning to say no and to step aside has been part of my faith experience because, I mean, I think that God also requires me to think of, you know, to think of what I need as well.' An Anglican woman spoke of 'making a conscious effort' to put herself first and of needing 'people to say it's OK to do that', because putting other people first had been 'exemplified and held up in the Bible and through people through Christian history. And that doesn't make it easy for me to put myself first.'

While this last woman felt it was a straightforward Christian imperative to put others first, other women no longer believed that not considering themselves was what was required of them as Christians. However, they still experienced the conflict inherent in competing needs. 'There are times where I will say no to people . . . and I don't take on things that will stress me out', said a Catholic woman in her thirties, 'but a lot of the time I'll say yes to things because I know somebody needs my help, genuinely needs my help ... But you go through times of conflict where you think, am I being a yes person, because I'm a woman and I should do all these things?' A Presbyterian woman in her forties was very aware of the ongoing struggle: 'I no longer believe intellectually that as a woman I have to meet other people's needs all the time, but it is so deep in me that I still do it more than I should. And it is difficult because I do accept what Jesus said about servanthood ... but I also accept ... that you do have to have a self of your own to give up ... and it's something I still struggle with ... and I find it not a place where my faith helps me. I find it a place where my faith hinders me, but it isn't the real faith, it's the warped version of it that I have been handed down.'

The move to self-consideration is often accompanied by a concern of taking this 'too far'. 'I was brought up with the whole attitude of to give and not to count the cost', said a Catholic woman in her fifties, 'and I think I have begun to move away from that and the tension within myself now is how I can be saying, hold it, I need to look after myself. And it's how I don't fall into the totally selfish attitude where everything must revolve around my needs and, on the other hand, I must recognise my own needs ... It's a tension and it's like a seesaw. Some days I don't look after my needs at all and other days I do, so it's a constant tension.'

This dilemma is not purely theoretical or without substantial consequences. A number of women spoke of their health being affected and of wearing themselves out in serving others and having to learn that they could not always meet everyone's needs. 'I think I've only just got to the point where I realise that if I don't meet my own needs I won't stay sane', explained a Methodist woman. 'I think I've spent too long meeting the needs of other people.' A Catholic woman voiced something similar: 'I always would have met everybody else's needs but my own. And I'm only now recognising [that] ... giving myself time is something I need to do. Something I never allowed myself the luxury of . . . and if I don't . . . my body's going to crack up.' Another Catholic woman put it like this: 'If your own needs aren't met I think it's very bad for you physically and mentally and spiritually, it's very bad. Because I mean you're a person and you've all the human frailties of that person.'

In all of this 'negotiation', women remain selves-in-relation. This is not about withdrawing from social interaction or responsibility.[39] But, as one Catholic woman in her fifties recognised, looking after themselves was the first way women could actually be of help to others. She had come to realise that taking on board her own psychological and emotional needs 'would actually work towards the doing of what God wanted me to be and do in a particular situation and would not be mitigating against it'.

The obvious dilemmas, struggles and tensions women experience in trying to negotiate between competing needs do not occur in some kind of neutral space without an existing social agenda. The difficulty women have in being true to their identities as selves-in-relation, that is in valuing both themselves and others, is that the dominant masculinist paradigm that orders public and private worlds understands such mode of being as 'feminine'. As such, society (and Christian institutions) operates with this understanding on an ideological (including theological) and practical level. So the self-worth that women find in their own understanding of God occurs in a context which constantly works to undermine that self-value by the expectations on women to put others before themselves. How, then, do we find a way out of this dilemma?

Self-respecting identities

In order for a society to value a relational mode of being and caring responsibilities, the gendered public/private division must itself be challenged. Care no longer must be seen as only appropriate for the so-called private realm, any more than justice should be viewed as relevant only in the public domain. Therefore, this is not about a choice between care and justice. Rather, it is that caring relationships should be just and issues of justice should foster positive relationships. Mary Stewart van Leeuwen argues that a biblical notion of justice concerns relationships between people and is part of a biblical vision of *shalom* or well-being that comes 'as an outgrowth of justice and love functioning in concert'.[40]

Working towards realising such a vision challenges any understanding and practice of gender relations that fosters women's subordination. This is not about dismissing sexual differentiation, that is, ignoring that humanity is female and male. Rather, it is to think about female and male identity in ways that maintain rather than work against sex equality. The position of gender complementarity is flawed because, operating along hierarchical gendered lines, women are subordinated in this to men. This is not to deny the possibility or even desirability of cooperation and instances of complementarity between women and men (or among persons of the same sex). But it is to say that if complementarity is viewed along gender lines, in the context of inequality, this will lead to a situation of dominance and subordination.

It may not be easy for us, but it is possible to think of maleness and femaleness in ways that do not place men and women in opposition to one another and, hence, lead to inequality. For example, Daphne Hampson's choice of the phrase 'neighbouring sex' rather than 'opposite sex' to describe gender relations is helpful here.[41] To talk of our 'neighbour' rather than our 'opposite' changes the nature of the conversation we are able to have when we think of ourselves as women and men. We do not have to talk of ourselves in ways that lead to value-laden gender stereotypes that diminish women's (or men's) full humanity. A synthesis of the various human characteristics currently allocated along gendered lines expresses human personhood, whether female or male, and this understanding is crucial to the idea of humanity made in the image of God. In other words, care, integrity, wisdom, relatedness, rationality, and love, to cite just a few human characteristics, are all expressions of human personhood, whether female or male. Saying this is not to talk about women appropriating a so-called masculine side of human nature or men a so-called feminine side. This perpetuates rather than confronts a dualistic gendered understanding of human existence. It is rather to talk about an integration of the various human characteristics in a person, what Rosemary Radford Ruether calls a 'psychic wholeness',[42] which partners the integration, suggested above, of a public and private social order. So for women to behave rationally, for example, is not for them to display their masculine side – it is part of their humanity for 'all humans possess a full and equivalent human nature and personhood, *as male and female*'.[43]

An example of how this understanding has the potential to transform relationships is illustrated by one woman describing the dynamic that currently operates during arguments with her husband. Speaking of times when he would become aggravated and use language like 'where did you pluck this from?' to respond to her argument, she remonstrated, 'It's something to do with you being a woman, you're being emotional. I was just being logical and I know with other men too that the more you say the more it's like you're proving them right – they've wiped you off just because you're a woman even though you know you've your arguments clearly laid out and you're calm . . . all this person is looking at is a woman.' With an integrated view of human personhood 'looking at a woman' can no longer be an excuse for assuming emotionalism and irrationality.

For Christian women an identity rooted in the notion of humanity, male and female, created in the image of God, offers the opportunity to explore the potential of humanness with the transformation that this can bring to both personal and social life. This does not mean, of course, that issues surrounding the conflicting needs described above simply evaporate! The development of self and society that a relational rather than oppositional vision of persons enables is a process that inevitably is fraught with difficulty. However, without this alternative vision women will continue to be disempowered and exploited by a dualistic social ordering which ultimately undermines all human personhood.

Chapter 4

DEFYING DESTINY AND EMBRACING BIOLOGY: *Women, social status and physicality*

It bothered people that I wasn't married. 'Why is she not married, there must be something wrong with her?'

Protestant woman under forty

I feel in some instances that I'm viewed as being less of a complete woman because I'm single and I've no children. And I know that that view exists within the church and I'm conscious of that all the time.

Catholic woman in her thirties

[The church] . . . said to me, you're a woman, you as a woman who is married, your function in life is to have babies, stay at home look after them . . . and that's what your life is supposed to be because that's what God wants your life to be, that's who you are in Christ.

Presbyterian woman in her forties

Is it not strange that women who give birth cannot bless the child of their womb, or other wombs?

Anne Thurston

Both marriage and motherhood are central to the way in which women view themselves and are viewed by others. While it sounds like a contradiction, women's identity as wives and mothers can be both affirming for *and* detrimental to them. This happens when marriage and motherhood, along with false notions about these experiences, become the sole means of definition for women either by themselves or others. It is important to understand how these potentially invaluable life experiences can be used to undermine all women, whether or not they are married or are mothers, and hence why, in terms of the way they are defined, women need to defy their so-called destiny.

TO BE OR NOT TO BE – MARRIED?

Many women who were or had at one time been married spoke warmly of their marriage relationship and of its importance to them. '[God] has taught me so much through marriage . . . that's been so precious', said a Presbyterian woman in her forties. 'He's taught me a lot about relationship with God . . . The whole willingness to be ourselves, warts and all, to be totally open, the loving developing relationship. I mean, we just felt we were so happy when we were married and yet that has just grown and developed . . . it just gets better and better and better . . . and to me that's just the same as the relationship with God, and that's his love, [my husband] loves me even with all the things I do and say wrong, and I'm the same with him. And so all that to me reflects the marriage relationship with Christ and the church.' For a Catholic woman, 'Some of my most spiritual experiences would have been in the context of my marriage and in the church . . . I would have experienced a real sense of Catholicism, of marriage being a sacrament, a sign of God . . . And of marriage as a symbol of Christ's unity . . . that was very deeply meaningful to me. Sex, you know, the whole idea of a sexual relationship, you know, being of God.' Another Catholic woman spoke of the spirituality of a married couple as 'loving one another. And the simple things we [do] is our spirituality. How I'm spiritually is how I am with [my husband] and [the] rest of [the] family . . . an awareness that God is there. It's like the Celtic spirituality where they were constantly aware of God in everywhere.'

These women spoke of deep and meaningful relationships with their husbands, reflecting the human need for love and connection and demonstrating that, at least for some, '"Bonds" are not just fetters; they are also lifelines.'[1] Further, for these Christian women, their marital relationships are part of their encounter with God. As such there is no division between this expression of their human and social embodiment and their spirituality. Rather, their spirituality finds meaning in their spousal relationships.

The value married women place on their marriages is echoed in the expression of their feelings towards their single friends who wanted to be married. 'I'm sad for my friends who aren't married', said an Anglican woman, 'because they would make wonderful wives and mothers and they would love to be married.' Another woman voiced a similar sentiment: 'There are some rare souls who can somehow come to terms with it and appreciate that God can use them and give them a fulfilled and satisfied life as a single person, but the majority of my single friends would dearly love to be married and have children . . . I do believe he meant men and women to be in a married relationship and support each other, be complementary, equal but different.' A Protestant woman in her sixties who had married when she was older and who was now a widow thought some single people tried to pretend they do not want to get married and that 'they don't need men, and I think it's more important to say that this is a gap in my life which God will help me live with – like the situation I'm in – rather than I don't need a man'.

These three women reflect three assumptions about women who are not married: that most women *want* to get married; that women *need* to be married; and that for single women God acts as a substitute for a husband. The difficulty with each of these assumptions is that they contribute to the diminishment of *all* women because they undermine women as full and equal human persons in their own right. How does this happen?

What women want?

Let's consider the assumption that most women want to get married. The difficulty in this statement is not in the accuracy of what it affirms, for it may well be true of Christian women in Northern Ireland, and indeed elsewhere. Rather, the problem is with the statement's emphasis on *most* women's aspiration, which leaves concealed the fact that *not all* women want to get married. 'I've never had any desire to be married, believe it or not, you know', said a Catholic woman in her sixties, 'I love the freedom of, you know, doing what I wanted . . . The old thing would have been you were left on the shelf, as it were. The funny thing was I never felt that way. Other girls it would have tortured them, they would have had to have been married, you know, and all that. I just always felt, I don't know, I just always felt that I was just a child of God and it didn't matter if you were married or not.'

The structural inequalities that women face in their family situations can play a part in women's reluctance to be married. 'For a long time I didn't want to get married because I was having a ball', said a Catholic woman now engaged to be married. 'I saw all [the responsibility] that . . . went with family life and I saw this curb on my freedom and just on things that I could do or maybe wanted to do and so I wasn't really interested in it. I felt that I would be the loser, if I got married I would be the loser. The husband gained as far as I was concerned, the wife became a mother eventually, eventually was the loser. And so I wasn't that interested at all. And also because I was happy with what I was doing . . . I didn't feel that I needed a man to complete me or complete my life.'

The tendency to conceal the fact that not all women want to get married means that marriage is viewed as the normative option for women and, hence, to not marry becomes seen as somehow 'odd', and the single person herself becomes the problem. As a Presbyterian woman remarked, 'Singleness is quite a big issue for me because I think the older you get the more people sort of look at you and think, "Good grief, you're not going out with anybody, you're not engaged, what's wrong with you?" And I think you question your own character.' Another woman spoke of similar pressure largely imposed by others: 'There are certain things that I've had to come to terms with, you know, like the fact that I'm thirty-three and single, which, especially in church circles, people have this lovely idea that because they are happily married everybody else has to be happily married and there's always this kind of, oh I know the perfect person for you . . . which you then have to come to terms with, you know. It's almost an issue that's forced on you by – well, I feel is forced on you by other people.'

The mixed message that the church conveys to unmarried women was observed by another single woman: 'This is the ironic thing, you don't get it so much in secular society but in Christian society where they talk about celibacy, and they talk about, you know, rights and gifts of people and . . . this calling to be single . . . in practice they don't believe it because they think you're a weirdo, you know. They think if you're single there must be something wrong with you, poor girl, on the shelf. Or "I wonder what her problem is?" Not that she's waiting for the right man, *waiting* being the operative word, but, you know, that there must be something emotionally unstable about her.'

Each of these comments reflects that among the currently single women who talked of their single status, their major preoccupation was with the difficulties they encountered from others because they were not married. Whatever their own concerns in regard to not being married, the pressure they felt from family, friends and society was an overriding issue. Their single status was viewed not with acceptance but as 'weirdo', 'something wrong', 'emotionally unstable'.

What women need?

That remaining single is viewed as abnormal is further endorsed by the second assumption, namely that women have a need to be married. While not disputing there may be difficult issues that some or even many women face because they are not married, the idea that women *need* to be married assumes women's fullest definition and selfhood comes through being married. It rehearses the view of women as those whose primary responsibility is the care and nurture of others, first and foremost in the context of their family. As a Presbyterian woman noted, 'society puts pressure on you even if you are going with somebody, like when you getting engaged? When you getting married? When's your children, when's your grandchildren?' An Anglican woman had faced the same presumption from her employers: 'They'd come out with horrendous things that women should stay in the home and "listen dear, listen dear, I've nothing against you personally, dear, but I think all this women going out to work stuff is . . .".'

With marriage as the 'institution which traditionally provides women with a social identity'[2] the absence of marriage robs women of social place. One woman reflected on the infantilisation of herself as a single woman: 'In some ways I struggle with the image of being a mature woman . . . I still would feel that I'm a child, you know, and I still feel as if I'm treated as a child. I think it's the singleness and I know with talking to other single friends they feel this quite strongly – you haven't been initiated, you haven't actually attained something . . . I do feel people treat me like a [child]. I'm continually being called a "wee girl" and also people saying, oh you're young – I'm middle aged! I mean, I don't want to admit it myself but, you know, this maturity thing . . . that really gets to you.'

God as substitute husband?

The idea that marriage signifies a maturity for women, that it makes them adult persons, suggests that a woman's adult status comes in relationship to a man and not on the basis of a woman's own self-development or identity. Hence, the first two assumptions that women both want and need to be married relate to the third assumption that women need to depend on God because they lack a marriage relationship. Interestingly, the women who in the main commented on their attitude towards God in regard to being single were those who are now married and who were looking back at how they had viewed their single status at the time. One currently single woman encapsulates their thinking: 'I think there has been a correlation between the idea of "marriage" or "not marriage and God", you know.'

Inherent in the idea of 'marriage' or 'not marriage and God' is an endorsement of the God – man – woman hierarchy, which places women in a subordinate relationship to men, seeing this as natural and God-ordained. In the absence of marriage women's need for God is seen to be greater to make up for what she as a single woman lacks, namely the ability to exist as a single female adult. It suggests that women need to rely either on a husband or, in his absence, on God. This denial of women's full adult status is another example of a gendered application of Christian theology. In the same way (as explored in chapter three) that Christian self-denial is applied differently according to gendered cultural notions and structures, the understanding of the Christian's reliance upon God is applied differently for women than for men. Dependence upon God for men does not detract from their autonomy and self-definition as social adults. In contrast, dependence upon God is required for women because they lack the ability to live as autonomous adults as selves-in-relation. This is not to say that there can be no value for single people of the affirmation of God in the absence of that which might be expected from a spouse. However, this does not have to be understood in a gender-specific way. As one woman explained, 'I think the understanding I came to that helped me wasn't particularly specific to women or to single people. I believe that we all have to find our completeness in God and, you know, I think that's as true for married people as for single people. But I think it's particularly helpful for single people. I don't know, it was just this coming to a point where I was just content, you know, in God's love . . . we all need other people at times but, you know, generally being content with just God's love and not really needing to strive for love or for, you know, affirmation anywhere else.' This understanding of God subverts a God – man – woman hierarchy and as such, while it involves, it does not confine women's spirituality to her marital status.

Defining women primarily as those who *should* be married (which logically is supported in the idea that women want to be married) and, hence, who particularly need God in the absence of a spouse, undermines women because it denies them full adult status as autonomous selves-in-relation. It is not that marriage in itself is the problem, nor is the desire for the intimacy, love, security, companionship or adventure that marriage potentially can be.[3] Rather, it is the prescribing of women's identity first and foremost as wives to the extent that single women face the pressures and discrimination described above, which diminishes all women. Married women themselves may not be affected directly by such attitudes, for many comply with social expectations. However, this view of women undermines all women because it restricts the concept of womanhood, curtailing women's self-definition and self-expression, and has practical discriminatory outcomes. While affirming marriage, therefore, it is the use of marriage to confine women to gendered norms that is at issue. A similar dynamic exists in relation to motherhood.

WOMEN'S EMBODIMENT: WITH AND WITHOUT CHILDREN

Similar assumptions exist about women as child-bearers as about women and marriage. Motherhood is viewed as normative for women, with child-bearing 'the supreme route to physical and emotional fulfilment'.[4] Motherhood is viewed as needed by women, this being further supported by children needing their mothers.[5] This means that, '[r]egardless of whether women become mothers, motherhood is central to the ways in which they are defined by others and of their perceptions of themselves'.[6] In disputing that women's physicality, 'their possession of ovaries and wombs',[7] means women have a need to be mothers, Ann Oakley has argued that along with the sexual division of labour, the idea of motherhood as women's natural and ultimate fulfilment is a myth that perpetuates women's subordinate status. Further, she argues that motherhood is socially constructed, that girls are socialised to want children.[8] While not disputing the social control over women through marriage and motherhood, nor that not all women do or should want children, a Christian understanding which finds theological resonance with the creativity of God in the experience of child-bearing and rearing, sees the creation and nurture of children as part of being human, and as such among the possibilities of what it means to be in the image of God.

The difficulty remains that our bodily experience is always 'culturally constructed and mediated'[9] and it is, therefore, not possible to isolate any pure culturally unmediated desire for children from its context of inequalities. However, Adrienne Rich's distinction between the experience of motherhood, 'the *potential relationship* of any woman to her powers of reproduction and to children' and the institution of motherhood 'which aims at ensuring that that potential — and all women – shall remain under male control' is useful here.[10] It affirms women as child-bearers/mothers while acknowledging the inequalities in which this potential experience exists.

What part does motherhood play in women's self-understanding and in perpetuating their subordination? In terms of women's identity, there is a need to affirm the experience of motherhood (the reality rather than any romanticised notion) while not allowing motherhood to become women's ultimate definition. In this regard, the title phrase of this chapter 'embracing biology' is not a reduction of motherhood to a single dimension. Rather, in the light of a romanticised, idealised concept of motherhood, it is used here to refer to the denied realities of both the physicality and practicalities of motherhood and also as an affirmation of the experience of motherhood for theological reflection. 'Defying destiny' is a satirical reference to women's supposed ultimate purpose in child-bearing. The irony is, of course, that those who purport that child-bearing is women's destiny often have had an ambivalent and even hostile attitude towards women's particular physicality and biological processes involved in child-bearing.

The idea of woman as mother

Let's think about the issues around the identification of women as mothers. The interviewees in this book consist of women who are mothers (including those who have fostered or adopted children) and women without children. There are a number of different experiences among women without children. They may be voluntarily childless, or childfree, having chosen not to have children. (This does not mean they do not face social pressures or assumptions, however, and are usually viewed as selfish.) They may have experienced pregnancy or child loss and remain without children. They may be infertile or part of an infertile couple who remain childless.[11] Women without children also include those who would dearly love to have children, but who are not in a situation whereby this can be contemplated, for Christian women this would generally be those who are not married. Fifteen of the interviewees spoke about infertility, childlessness, child loss and pregnancy loss and they included single women who clearly viewed the possibility of having children as dependent upon a married relationship. The phrase 'women without children' incorporates all these experiences and highlights the focus here for, while each situation contains its own particularities, the difficulty of making motherhood women's primary definition affects all women, whether mothers or not and in all circumstances of not being mothers.

The mothers interviewed spoke warmly and lovingly, as well as realistically, about their children, their relationships with them and their experiences of motherhood. The ability to know close intimate relationships with their children of which many of the women spoke is one of the attractions and benefits of motherhood.[12] Motherhood also provides women with social status and adult identity. As one woman remarked, 'I think from the point of view of identity, having children helped because I felt, I think it is the most creative thing a woman can do . . . It definitely gave me more of an identity and . . . it gave me a certain authority.'

The difficulty with the positive endorsement to women's identity that comes with being a mother is not so much in what it affirms as it is in the restriction of women's validation to motherhood (which for the woman just quoted is suggested in her description of having children as 'the most creative thing a woman can do'). When motherhood becomes women's primary definition, for those women without children, such positive endorsements of women become negative identities. This is reflected partly in the terminology to describe women without children (whether from their own choice or not). 'The terms for childlessness, like infertile, barren and sterile, are derogatory, implying a failure not merely in reproductive terms but as women. The lives of childless women are seen as empty, lacking the fulfilment and warmth motherhood brings.'[13]

It is among women without children in particular that there is an acute awareness of this negative identity which, for Christian women, is endorsed by their churches. Two women, a Presbyterian in her forties and a Catholic woman in her thirties, reflected at length on this:

> [The church] . . . said to me, you're a woman, you as a woman who is married, your function in life is to have

babies, stay at home, look after them, make [cakes] for the church, maybe help in the crèche, you can sing in the choir and you might be able to do a bit of praying, but not too high profile. And that's what your life is supposed to be because that's what God wants your life to be, that's who you are in Christ. Although it wasn't often put together as coherently as that, those were the messages, I'm convinced of that . . . And then when you have friends . . . who start to do it and they start to be the things that the church wants them to be and you really want to be too but can't, then you've got a big problem . . . I think that to say that to a woman whether she's married, single or whatever she is, is dreadful, it is just appalling, and it is a disinheritance and it is a denial of herself in Christ because that is where the meaning is. And stuff them, you know, it's not about roles . . . it's not about all that stuff, it's dreadful, dreadful, so it was unhelpful even before then but it got compounded . . . once we started trying to have babies and they didn't appear, whatever was bad before that became, it was like multiplication tables, it was an exponential curve because then you're into issues that nobody can deal with, you see.

I feel in some instances that I'm viewed as being less of a complete woman because I'm single and I've no children and I know that that view exists within the church and I'm conscious of that all the time . . . Also I feel that too many of my friends marry because it's what they think they should do – not because it's the person they want to spend their life with, but because it's the person who was around and available and marry for all the wrong reasons. It's not only social pressure but also church pressure. Within the Catholic Church it's still very – a lot of fundamentalist thinking – a woman's role is to get married and to have children. I don't mean that in the sort of Dark Ages role, but you know what I mean. There is a sense of you're not

> complete until you're married and have children and I struggle with that. I mean, I struggle with that in the sense of, not that I wouldn't, that I would say I never want to be married or I never want to have children, but it's not my life. It's not how my life is, it's not the situation I find myself in so there's no point in me wishing my life away or me thinking well, I should work towards this . . . I have too many friends who have done that, gone down that road and who are not happy and who have had children . . . married for the wrong reasons, totally the wrong reasons and I don't want to do that.

Both of these women encapsulate the difficulties women without children face in a context which understands women's primary definition as that of wife/mother. Another woman expresses how she overcame viewing child-bearing and mothering as her primary identification and validation: 'I remember thinking that I will have to accept and grasp onto this that God loves me as a person, as myself, I don't need to be a mother to be useful and to, I suppose there's a bit of me that I need to be useful, I need to be able to do something, I need to feel I have achieved something. And I can remember thinking, nearly letting go of this yearning to have a family, and saying right God you can use me, I can be a very worthwhile person without a family.'

This does not mean there is no loss involved in being without children. The women who spoke about not having children talked in terms of the grief, loss and bereavement that being childless was to them. Enabling women to have a larger self-definition than child-bearing and motherhood does not mean that women do not experience the devastation of being childless. The point, rather, is that viewing women primarily as child-bearers and mothers restricts all women in their human potential and, indeed, exacerbates the enormous personal difficulties that involuntarily childless women face. For motherhood as woman's primary role imposes a definition on womanhood which some women will never realise. As such, perpetuating a notion of motherhood as ultimate fulfilment is to diminish women who never become mothers, viewing them with a negative rather than a positive identity. Further, it denies their full humanity in its refusal to acknowledge their embodiment as those without children.

The reality of woman as mother

Making motherhood woman's primary definition imprisons all women because it is accompanied by an idealised concept of motherhood. This romanticised view hides the experience of child-bearing and rearing and, in so doing, places an additional burden on women with children to live up to an unrealistic ideal. The myth involves the idea that women naturally know how to mother and enjoy the experience. A Methodist woman thought otherwise: 'It's having the responsibility to these children, I wasn't trained to look after them, I knew nothing about them. It was a total mystery. Of course I loved them, I wanted the best for them.' However, as Paula Nicolson points out, the 'romanticised and idealised woman, full of love, forgiveness and selflessness, does not and cannot exist, so that all mothers are destined to disappoint their children and themselves'.[14] As another woman commented about her church in respect of the difficulties she faced in bringing up her children, 'sometimes I think they [the church] specialise in illness and death, you know, you're allowed to be needy when something like that has happened but . . . it's not so good to be depressed or to have [other] difficulties – we didn't talk about rebellious children'.

To maintain that an idealised motherhood is unattainable is not to argue that women who mother do not often exhibit a selflessness that comes from being responsible for a child. As a Presbyterian woman commented, 'Things change completely I think once you've had a baby and you become a less selfish person. That was probably part of my leaving self behind and all of a sudden a baby, he took priority, the world revolved around him, it certainly did for me.' Indeed, it is the truth of mothers' experience that enables the myth of the selfless, perfect mother to be plausible. However, it is this idealising and romanticising of the mother role that is problematic because it hides the difficulties of bearing and raising children. For despite 'the prominence of motherhood as a social institution, and the almost universal expectation that women will become mothers, the everyday reality of mothering is frequently invisible'.[15]

Something of the everyday experience that mothering can be was articulated by one woman with six children: 'I felt as though my mind was going to blow, I really had given out too much, it was all give and I really felt as though my soul was starved.' Speaking of a three month period in which she arranged some time for herself she said, 'I sat down at the desk . . . I took an hour, one hour three times a week . . . for the first part of that I cried . . . just cried, and cried and cried . . . [Sometimes I] fell asleep I was so tired. The tears were frustration – I had all this creative energy inside, you know, and then I would write and I've kept all that stuff. I just wrote. I just wrote my feelings . . . stuff about being a woman and getting caught in this cycle of caring and caring and caring . . . that was one of the best things I ever did.' The physical and emotional work of mothering several children means that additional pregnancies exacerbate a mother's situation. As another woman recalled, 'I remember saying to God, you know, what are you doing, I cannot, cannot cope with any more children . . . I really thought there is no God, I really was angry.'

Motherhood as a 'bio-social process'[16] is a complex experience. Its hidden dimensions include the possibility of financial dependence (either on another person or the state), economic hardship, physical exhaustion, loss of control of time and energy, loss of control of one's own body in physical and mental/emotional well-being,[17] changes in interpersonal relationships and in domestic, occupational and sexual arrangements. Making these components visible is not a denial of the pleasure or delight that motherhood can be for women. Nor is it to suggest that these more difficult aspects of motherhood should be weighed against the deep satisfaction that having children can produce. But challenging the idealisation of motherhood is necessary because such romanticism imprisons all women by its false expectations and impossible demands.

While the idealisation of motherhood focuses more on the 'servicing activities'[18] required in caring for children, it has been more silent in regard to the physicality involved in child-bearing/rearing. This is partly due to the ambivalence and even hostility to human bodiliness in general and female bodiliness in particular in which women's association with physicality rather than reason and spirituality have rendered femaleness as antithetical to the divine. A vivid example of this was provided by a Catholic woman in a religious order, now in her sixties, speaking of the ways she was instructed to conduct herself: 'Once you entered [religious life] you got this veil – you never came out without putting a towel over your head if you wanted to go to the toilet from your little cubicle . . . You were never supposed to appear in public without a towel over your head . . . You never had a bath without wearing this chemise thing that you were given to cover your body, 'cos you weren't supposed to see your body, you know, all of those things. I found all those things terribly foreign because I wasn't used to them . . . I never wore that thing. I used to take it into the bath with me and wring it out as if I used it, but I never used it. There was always something within me that I knew that this was not of God. Nobody told me and everybody was telling me the opposite, but there was something within me, and this is where the grace of God and God was sort of, I feel, always with me, there was always this little voice in me saying, that's OK.'

While this may be considered an extreme example, it reveals a negative attitude towards women's bodies that still exists and, hence, an impoverished notion toward embodiment. The idea evident throughout history that women's bodiliness is 'unclean'[19] has left a legacy of uneasiness with regard to the physiological processes of menstruation, pregnancy, childbirth, and breast-feeding of which child-bearing consists.[20] Of course, if we begin to place an emphasis on the physicality of child-bearing, this could be used to perpetuate the association of women with human bodiliness in contrast to masculine experience more focused on rational abstraction. We need to remember, therefore, that a focus on women's physicality seeks to address the exclusion of the bodily realities of child-bearing from the idealised model of motherhood. It does not imply, however, that attention to embodiment is only for mothers or women in contrast to male experience. Elaine Graham states, 'There is an urgent need for dominant, privileged groups to become critical about their own racial, sexual and gender identity, and begin to make it possible for everyone to think from the Body; or else bodily experience is restricted to a property of those speaking from a position of "difference", which in practice means the abnormal, problematic, victimized body. It is therefore essential that embodiment is affirmed as a common human trait, even though our experiences may be diverse and characterized by inequality of representation, access to resources and self-determination.'[21]

A focus on the social/physical realities of motherhood is needed in order to combat a romanticised notion of motherhood that imprisons women. What is more, it is in the reality not the idealisation that theological resonance is found.

Mother as theological resource

'Childbirth was a very precious experience of God's creation', said a Presbyterian woman. 'It gave me a sense of, "God you're so awesome". I looked at [my daughter's] finger nails, every detail and I thought you've made that, and all the workings inside her.' This woman is expressing how the experience of childbirth itself speaks to her of God. An Anglican recalled childbirth as the time she had most intensely glimpsed the joy of God: 'Childbirth bought me quite close to God in terms of all sorts of feelings about joy and good feelings that I had never experienced before and the whole notion of creation. And I don't know that I really thought about those at the time, but when you reflect upon them afterwards, now I know that, particularly the birth of my first child, I remember this sense of joy and then relating that somehow to God. An experience that I haven't experienced at any other stage. A feeling, and knowing that God . . . has that feeling or that that's part of creation, that's part of God's creation – God as creator must have this feeling of joy in the same way as I as a mother had that feeling of joy . . . That was the only time I have ever felt it just as strongly.'

This sense of God, this glimpse of the divine, described by a Catholic woman as 'a holy sense [of] the awe and the wonder of creation', comes not only from the presence of a newly born child, but also from the experience of giving birth itself. Speaking of very difficult and unexpected pregnancies which had happy outcomes another woman reflected, 'somebody told me once that you never forget the person who delivers your baby, you know, the physical person. And, you know, you always have fond memories of the doctor or midwife or whatever and, you know, I look back and I do think . . . fondly of this man who delivered my baby. But I think that because God was such a central part in the conception and delivery of my children, I think that, you know, you never forget what God meant to you at that stage and in fact God takes on a completely new, I don't know, dimension. To me he did anyway.' When the suggestion was put to her that this was 'God the midwife, almost?', she replied, 'Yes that's right, that's the idea of the femininity in God sort of thing . . . Life will never be the same again after that.'

As discussed earlier, viewing women's experience as illustrative of a 'feminine' side to God perpetuates a dualistic gendered understanding of humanity which contributes to women's subordination. However, to say this does not deny this woman's experience nor undermine the meaning she finds in it. God was involved in her female embodied experience of pregnancy and birth and through that became real and known to her in a way she had not experienced before. While affirming such encounter and meaning, it is possible to advocate a different analytical framework in which to set both her experience and its meaning. As Elaine Graham notes, one 'cannot simply assume that once women start telling their stories they will instantly shed the false illusions of patriarchal accounts and emerge, free of oppression, as the tellers of completely authentic, totally self-actualized narratives. The transition from silence to speech is never easy.'[22] In the absence of other interpretative frameworks, women probably understand their experiences along patriarchal models. But this woman's experience of 'God the midwife' can be viewed as a reflection of divinity in its fullness and not simply a so-called feminine side of the divine. Sallie McFague argues that the metaphor of God as mother speaks not only of God as life-giver and creator but as judge, bringing together the idea of motherly nurture and justice for '[t]hose who produce life have a stake in it and will judge, often with anger, what prevents its fulfillment'.[23]

For many women even the notion of child-bearing as a theological resource may have to be learned. A Catholic mother of six children commented, 'Childbirth in itself could have the potential of an immense kind of spiritual, spiritual and sexual experience. I think I was kind of seeing the potential for that whenever I finished.' An Anglican woman spoke on how unexpected the spirituality experienced in motherhood was: 'I was quite a career person . . . and had always looked after various cousins and whatnot and childbirth to me wasn't going to be any big deal, if you like, and I sort of wasn't prepared for how big a deal it was . . . Just watching your children grow up, you know, reminds me of the way God watches us and how much he has put into us and how much I have put into my children. And the fact that how much you love them, but you have to let them – you can teach them all that you like, but you still have to let them make their own mistakes. I think that has helped me. I mean it's a very simple thing, but it has helped me understand how God lets things happen . . . And also I just have two children, but the fact, you know, they are two totally different children and that I feel as much for each of them, you know, that I don't have more love for one than another, if you like, but it's a different sort of love . . . I can't imagine having all the children that there are in the world, but, I mean, God can deal with it.'

A Christian notion of humanity made in the image of God enables the possibility of the experience of child-bearing and rearing to be sources of theological reflection. And clearly motherhood is a resource for theological reflection. 'I understood so much more about God as father when I realised what my attitude was to [my daughter]', said an older Protestant woman, 'because I was not condemning her for not being able to walk or talk or do things before she was able to. I was simply delighted with every new thing she did and I realised that God loved me at the stage I was at and he was pleased when I developed as a person . . . If [my daughter] had done something she shouldn't have done, when she had apologised, I didn't want her going on being upset about it, I wanted our relationship restored immediately. I wanted us to be happy together and I saw that God did not want me going on being miserable over something I had done once it was forgiven.'

Some of these experiences of motherhood, while more typical in our society of women, potentially may be experienced by either parent. While the 'female experience of gestation, birth and lactation'[24] is peculiar to women, other aspects of parenthood need not be. However, viewing motherhood in particular as a source of theological reflection is important because, against a background of neglect of female imaging of the divine, it counters the view that women and their experiences (of which motherhood is a part) are unsuitable vehicles for speaking of the divine. Using female God-talk alongside male God-talk is a reminder of the limited nature of all language for God. It also exposes the sexuality hidden in male metaphors – male imaging is not asexual.[25] Hence, utilising motherhood as a source of theological reflection, by which both women and men may understand God, would challenge Christian women's current devalued position that follows when God is imaged dominantly as male.

If women's bodily/social experience of motherhood can be viewed as a source of theological reflection,[26] what Elaine Graham describes as the way 'narratives of embodiment act as disclosure of divine reality and activity',[27] then there are implications for the life of the Christian community. As Anne Thurston states, 'Is it not strange that women who give birth cannot bless the child of their womb, or other wombs? . . . Women who nurture and feed their children initially from their own bodies and therefore who know what it is to give of their flesh to eat, cannot bless and break the bread which will nurture all the people. Women who attend to the sufferings of one another . . . are not permitted to bring God's healing and forgiveness to one another. Women who daily wash the bodies of small children and of the sick and the elderly are not called to wash the feet of one another as a witness to such service – or even more oddly are not permitted to have their feet washed at the Holy Thursday liturgy. Women in their lives and in their work image God and image Christ; what we need now are the visible signs of this imaging in all the structures of the church.'[28]

The consequences of taking women's experience of motherhood seriously are far-reaching. To do so would be evidence that Christian women are full and equal members of their faith communities.

Chapter 5

'SUBORDINATED INSIDERS': *Women and the church*

I think women just seem not to be part of the church at all, you know. I mean, in our church we have women on the vestry, but I feel that they're not taken seriously . . . The women aren't taken seriously enough and I think that women's experience isn't taken seriously enough . . . I think women aren't valued and I just think they've so much to give.

Anglican woman in her forties

I think that women are greatly undervalued in our church and I think that it's a shame. I think it's shameful, not just a shame.

Catholic woman in her twenties

I see a lot of women involved in the church. It's the role *in which women are involved in the church . . . There is this understanding, unsaid, unspoken understanding of where the limits are, you know. And there's always this sort of thinking, or perception, that thus far and no further do women go.*

Presbyterian woman in her forties

Christianity is rooted in community remembrance and tradition. Intrinsic to it is the notion of a faith community to which people belong. Church institutions, however, are organised along gendered, hierarchical lines and women's experience, therefore, is that of 'subordinated insiders'.[1] Women are insiders in so far as they adhere to the practices and much of the ethos of the institutions, but women are subordinated in this to men.

THE 'BACKBONE' OF THE CHURCH

A clear indication of women's subordinated reality is the lack of value placed on their church participation. Women's considerable involvement in church institutions is probably one of the few indisputable elements surrounding women and church. It is widely recognised that church women are very active in and committed to the various denominations. The words of an Anglican woman convey the general sense expressed by most of those interviewed: 'I think women are the backbone of the church, quite honestly. I think they're the bulk of the attenders and everything and the strength of the church.'

There is, however, a sexual division that exists in churches. The picture is of lay women being the majority in attendance, sustaining much of the overall ministry and activity of an individual congregation by their practical support and presence. Yet rarely are women involved in terms of equal or even notable numbers within denominational church structures at congregational leadership level (either in terms of government or public worship). Consequently, they are also under-represented at denominational level. In summary, the majority of women's lay involvement in the churches is concerned with a variety of 'low status' tasks that are more often considered women's domain. Much of this is the 'housework' role and responsibility for children that women typically occupy outside of the churches; much of it being unseen.

The sense of not being valued was articulated by women across the denominations and ages. Women spoke of wanting 'more acknowledgement of what women do' and of the need for 'them to be more encouraged to do more'. They wanted to see women 'given more respect, higher status, being more appreciated'. They felt that church had lacked 'energy and purpose' in isolating rather than 'availing of the giftedness' of women; that church had 'denied the experience, the ministry, the value of women'; and that women's proper inclusion would 'create a freshness' that is badly needed. Women considered they were 'undermined and undervalued and patronised, a little pat on the head and keep doing the good work and making the tea'. They felt that male leaders gave the appearance of listening to women and taking them seriously, but this was 'a make believe thing'.

Even among women who hold a view that assigns overall leadership to men only, there exists a sense that women's contribution is not valued sufficiently by the church, as does a desire for women's greater involvement within the existing frameworks. So, a Protestant woman in her fifties commented, women would still do their traditional roles of catering and cleaning, but 'there are other things we can do'. She expressed her great difficulty in being in a home-group led badly by a man knowing 'there are three women that could do it far more profitably'. Moreover, she saw within her existing theological framework (of divinely ordained male authority) the possibility of accommodating this, but 'what I cannot accept is when the men who have this authority won't use that as a means of rubber stamping the ministry of women in certain areas'. This woman and others have a strong sense of women's abilities and talents being neglected. They are unhappy being excluded from the 'decision-making of the church', which is 'far too male dominated', and 'don't like the image of women being subservient'.

A feminist engagement with Christianity poses a greater challenge to church institutions than the thinking of those who want a greater inclusion of women while supporting male hierarchies. This is because recognising and affirming the value of women is about challenging, in the words of a Catholic woman in her fifties, 'the whole patriarchal thing and . . . I would have a lot of disappointment with our church for the control [men] have been exercising over the years.' Women's socialised position operates within church institutions as it does in the rest of society. 'I think it's all to do with upbringing and society as a whole', said a Presbyterian women over fifty. 'We would be inclined to think in our church, you see, that women, they're not to be pushing forward and doing the men's jobs and that kind of thing. Perhaps we're inclined to think that we should keep our place.' Another woman agrees: 'There's been so much conditioning over the years and you just assume, oh well, the men will do that or that is how it is so, therefore, we don't question, we just go along. And it frustrates me and it annoys me to see that there's some very capable women and they just don't take on things because they feel they're inadequate or they feel they've nothing to contribute. Yet they have a lot of spiritual maturity and a lot of experience, so I find that sad.' These comments highlight the fact that while women *may* be involved in a variety of ways in many denominations and congregations, there is a dearth of active encouragement for them to do so. There is also an absence of robust affirmation that would help women overcome any lack of confidence in themselves and in the positive contribution they have to offer.

None of this yet mentions the direct conflict with their denomination that some women encounter specifically over their contribution *as women*. Incidents of 'walkout', verbal challenge and ostracism may be viewed as individual occurrences, and some of the women who spoke of such experiences also spoke of support received by others in their churches. Such instances, however, serve as a reminder of the strength of opposition that exists within church institutions to women's full participation. It may be that women are not present in leadership or public roles in sufficient numbers to produce this kind of antagonism on a larger scale.[2] There is, however, a widespread prevalence of an unfavourable and even hostile attitude to women that permeates church institutions. Commenting on the opposition she had received from some men in her local congregation, one woman said, 'There is an assumption that there is something inadequate in a woman or lacking in a woman and, you know, I think there are undercurrents . . . But the thing is, if you speak [about] them you're oversensitive or you've got a bit of chip on your shoulder.'

It may be that the often unfocused nature of the resistance (if not hostility) to women's full participation within church institutions is one reason to account for why many women express an acceptance of their church's attitude to women while others have difficulty in expressing full personhood within churches. Although it may be hard to identify, the dualistic gender hierarchy is at work. We have already seen how at the heart of dualism there is a valuing of one set of characteristics or attributes and an accompanying devaluing of those characteristics placed in opposition to these. The association of everything identified as masculine as being of value and that which is understood as feminine to be without or of lesser value is crucial in any assessment of women's participation in church institutions. The devaluing of women which occurs in both God-talk and issues surrounding personal identity, is also evident in churches and is reflected in women's absence or minority presence within the institutional structures.

MALE DOMINANCE AND MASCULINITY

Institutional church structures are male dominated. This is evident in the Catholic Church and those Protestant denominations that do not ordain women or admit them into leadership roles. However, it is true also of those institutions that do admit women into roles of governance, whether in a clerical or lay capacity. For in these situations women remain in a minority overall, despite in some cases a tradition of access that spans decades.[3]

The reasons for this latter situation are complex.[4] Among them is the reality of the social structures and expectations on women we have already looked at and return to below. It is also the case that not everyone within a denomination supports their institution's stance on women's participation. For example, in the Presbyterian Church in Ireland, where a minister does not support the idea of women elders, this in effect can bar women from ever attaining this position. So there are still congregations where women do not sit on the kirk session 'and where Ministers will openly claim that they do not support the election of women to the ruling eldership'.[5] One woman discovered this when choosing to vote for women in an eldership election in her congregation: 'I made the mistake of voting on a few women simply because they work so hard and so long. And my minister said, although you can vote, the electorate are there and include men and women, but really we only have male elders.'

The male dominance of the government of churches inevitably influences the way each institution carries out its various leadership, worship and pastoral functions, and its communal activities. 'I sit in church every Sunday,' said an Anglican woman, 'and there's five male clerics up the front and an all-male choir and completely exclusive language in the service, which is quite hard for me. To me inclusivity is one of the big issues and I think it's not there for me anywhere. I don't know if it's there in any Anglican church that I attend in this area.' Similarly, a Presbyterian woman noted, 'There are still Sundays where, you know, the minister does everything himself and where those on the door and lifting the offering happen all to be men. I think we always need to be aware of the impression that that gives.'

Such male dominance perpetuates an androcentric view of the world in which maleness is normative human experience. It also presents an androcentric view of women. A Catholic woman explains, 'I've been in chapel and heard the priest talking about . . . women's issues and things and, you know, abortion and stuff and I have serious problems with that. And [they talk] just in a really negative way [about women] and how women have to take care, you know, just to be mothers . . . I just have loads of problems with . . . men talking about what women should be doing.'

It is precisely this situation of male dominance with its accompanying attitudes towards women that gives rise to the call for women's greater involvement in church. For some, it is simply that, in the words of an Anglican woman, 'male and female are equal in the sight of God', a notion rooted in the understanding of humanity made in the image of God. Others stress the variety of gifts that women possess, which do not necessarily stereotype them to gender roles, and which could be for the benefit of the whole church. After all, said a Catholic woman in her sixties, church authorities are 'depriving half of the church of the gifts of the other half'. Some women express a belief in a special contribution that women have to offer. This special contribution is associated with a feminine side. This could be inherent to women, 'a special feminine . . . instinct . . . and intuition . . . that men don't accept'. Or it may arise out of female experience and 'the women's perspective on actually a lot of things round the family, the church and a lot of understanding which is vastly missing from males'. Often contrasted with men's capabilities, 'women have the gift of love and tenderness, or something different from men that men haven't got', this special contribution could also be seen not in opposition to, but in partnership with, that of men: 'men have wonderful gifts and women have wonderful gifts . . . I feel there's a lovely complementation'.

The difficulty with the idea of women's special contribution, as with the notion of gender complementarity discussed in chapter three, is that it perpetuates a dualistic framework within which human beings operate and organise themselves.

Even when seen as contributing to a partnership between women and men, associating characteristics such as compassion, tenderness and understanding with a feminine side does nothing to challenge the oppositional framework, which consistently devalues such attributes. Incorporating a largely missing 'feminine' element within church institutions through greater inclusion and involvement of women, who would bring the neglected attributes with them, may appear preferable to women's exclusion. However, it enables the core masculine nature of the institutions to remain unchanged, but with softening feminine sides added. In other words, rather than break down the gender barriers and hierarchy (and a masculinity that defines itself as separate from and superior to women), it keeps them in place.

An illustration of this comes from the Catholic Church and the opening up in the last decade of the possibility (if given permission by the bishop of a diocese[6]) of girls serving at the altar, something previously restricted to boys. There are now female altar servers, said one Catholic woman, 'only because they couldn't get the boys to keep going, you know, so they've actually said, well we'll have to broaden it out'. Not so, according to another Catholic. She thought it was allowing girls to be altar servers that was resulting in a reluctance of boys to fulfil this function 'because they think it's too sissy now to be on the altar'. While these explanations seem contradictory, they are not necessarily mutually exclusive. Both present a picture of masculinity that is constructed in opposition to femaleness. This masculinity is safeguarded either by the exclusion of women from various functions or by women's admission because of the withdrawal of men from those same spheres. The model of female exclusion rather than that of partnership or mutual co-operation belongs to an ethos that devalues female experience and expression in order to protect male identity. Hence, for one of these women, 'the tolerance of women in the Catholic Church is basically tokenism'.

Indeed, given the male dominance that continues to exist within church institutions those women who do participate often refer to the experience as tokenism.[7] Not only is there the lack of an equal or sometimes any female presence throughout institutional structures (from local to denominational level), there is also an attitude that pervades the institutions that has kept women excluded or with only minority representation for so long. As a woman from one of the larger Protestant traditions explained, 'It was really only when I went to [the church's governing meetings] that I became quite conscious of the power structures within our church and a bit disillusioned with some of the attitudes.' She spoke of 'the almost innate attitudes to women and the role of women in the church', becoming 'more aware of the absence of women in the decision-making bodies', and how in the governing structures of the church 'the women are just the token'. She recognised, 'I'm the token female, and it is intimidating because, well, you know, if one man was sitting in a group of women he would be intimidated.'

Within Protestant churches, the fact that women may stand for institutional office or apply for ordination but obviously do not do so in great numbers, is often cited as an end to the matter by those who resist any attempt at women's fuller integration in practice. However, while some women lack the self-confidence or self-legitimisation to put themselves forward for such leadership positions, this is by no means the whole story. For an invitation to do just this is akin to an invitation to join a men's club with its rules and regulations with little or no experience of operating within such rules, or knowledge of how to apply them. Moreover, as we shall now consider, it is an invitation to join an existing arrangement, be added or absorbed into an established institution, as opposed to working out how women and men might together organise themselves in ways in which they both have ownership, identity and purpose.

Clericalism and committees

'I look at myself, right, married [to an ordained minister], and I've had a family and I can't think that I could have done my husband's job as a mother and a wife.' These are the words of a Presbyterian woman who is happy for women to preach and for single women to become ordained. However, she has reservations about married women becoming ordained, as she explains: 'I think the roles [for a woman and a man] are very slightly different and defined by the society that we live in. I know there are quite a few women who are ministers and they seem to survive with looking after a home and bringing up a family, being a mother, and I think something must go. Something must go because I can't see how they can fulfil the type of role that [my husband] does because he's called out at all hours of the day and night . . . he's not just a nine to five minister. He has to be available if somebody needs him in the middle of the night, if somebody's in trouble he has to be able to go. So how do you do that when you are a mother unless you've got a very good baby-sitter round the corner? If your husband's getting up to do a job the next day — I think, I suppose I'm saying, alright, if you've a husband that stays at home and takes over the role of the mother and wife, maybe it works.'

For this woman, the needs of the ordained ministry conflict with the needs of being a wife and mother. Her only solution is to reverse the roles of husband and wife. She does not think in terms of challenging the nature or practice of ordained ministry. An Anglican woman, also married to a clergyman, sees things differently: 'I think [women] work in different ways. I think women don't as easily work in the hierarchical structure and I think if women were in there it would force the church to think and to live differently, the institutional church I'm talking about, you know. Because if a woman is a minister and has a child then you've got to think, you know, how many sessions a week is she going to work? Does she need to work seven days a week, three sessions a day? I think that in turn would help ministry in general . . . I think there are major things that need to be challenged and it doesn't need women to challenge them. I mean, men can challenge them, but I don't know that they will. I think women will and a lot of that's to do with gender and children and just the way they see things and the way they work and the way they prioritise in different ways.'

Where both these women agree is in their recognition that institutional church structures are inhospitable places for women. While the Presbyterian woman sees this as unavoidable, given society's assigned gender roles, the Anglican woman wants to change the nature of ordained ministry, not only for women participants, but for men and their families too.

However, the issue of women's inclusion in the governing bodies of the churches does not only concern questions of family responsibilities. Catholic women express reservations about women being ordained into a celibate priesthood (which would remove the pragmatic conflict between priesthood and motherhood)[8] because of the way ordained ministry is practised. As one woman commented: 'I would love to see women priests. I wouldn't want to see them within the structures they are in at the moment. I would want things to change.' This change is about 'bishops in particular' becoming more in touch with the people, using inclusive language, and lay people's participation in the life of the church, which would give a sense of belonging and transformation. For her, this would make the Eucharist celebration real, in that 'we may become what we say we receive', the body of Christ. This is what she would like to see women become a part of rather than the church as it currently operates. As another Catholic put it, 'I believe that where women are ordained, as in every other organisation, that you have to assimilate the organisation, you have to fit in to it and that in so doing you may well compromise, or you have to compromise. I mean, I experience it in my work. I operate in a very hierarchical organisation. Now it's up to me to decide whether I want to keep that job and hang on in there and adapt and adjust because you cannot just flout custom and regulations and everything else. It's the same for women priests.'

Working within the system is not easy for many women who are to be found within government structures. Speaking of being an elder on a Presbyterian Kirk session, one woman observed, 'Men do tend to dominate the business. Men know how committees and structures [work], that's men's things and that's how things still run and I don't know how you change that.' But if challenging the leadership dynamic in church institutions is difficult when attempted from *within*, from outside there is the hurdle of first gaining access to the people who make decisions. As a Presbyterian woman reflected, 'There isn't really the forum for expressing your ideas.' Her only option was to approach people within the congregation's government with whom she had some rapport: 'It's almost very subversive or something, you have to make your feelings known through these channels.' A Catholic woman felt that change was resisted by her church: 'I would like to be more involved in real discussion with parishioners. I feel an awful lot of work that goes on in our church is superficial and it stops short of real dialogue and part of me feels that the hierarchy doesn't want to rock the boat. They don't want the hassle that goes with real dialogue because then that changes people.'

To pay lip service to women's inclusion is one thing, to facilitate it in actual structures is another. Reflecting on the contradictory nature of her church, a Protestant woman noted, 'There are areas where they have encouraged women to develop gifts. Now they maybe don't always provide the opportunity and the structure in which you can do it in the context of the church.' In other words, the belief that God has 'made us a certain way, given us gifts, given us abilities, given us a particular type of personality, that all those things are there to be used to their fullest extent in God's service', does not translate into women's church participation. An Anglican woman expressed her frustration at the marginalisation of women within institutional structures: 'I have found the church uncooperative in that it's in favour of supporting [the] traditional women's role bit. It has to be through Mother's Union and it has to be done in a certain way and I'm not into that at all. I think it only seems to be able to support women in that way, it doesn't seem to know different ways.'

Examining institutional structures is not simply a theoretical issue, or intellectual exercise, on the grounds that it would be nice to be more inclusive in this day and age. Any institutional structure has power to do harm as well as good. In trying to articulate what her faith in God had meant for her as a female human being one woman said, 'Probably if I could fully incorporate it and take it outside of the damage that's been done by the hierarchical structures, it probably would be brilliant. My theory is great but the structures have left their mark. I've been brutally oppressed by males in many ways.'

The debate about institutions is important because the way they operate and the ethos and theology that undergird their structures affects all their members. It determines what is possible within the various churches. Identifying the masculine ethos not only in terms of dominance of numbers or exclusivity in leadership positions, but in the very way structures are exercised, is to raise the debate about how women and men might function together in their corporate Christian life. It is not about adding women but *asking new questions*. To challenge the existing way that denominational institutions operate is not to determine the outcome. Rather, it is to establish the need for dialogue that will allow a thorough examination of the ethos, rationale and practice of church institutional organisation in order that they are places hospitable to women's full personhood.

Silly or serious?

'It doesn't really matter to me', said an Anglican woman in her fifties, 'I do know it matters an awful lot to some people.' She is referring to the use of inclusive language when speaking of human beings in church contexts. A non-issue for herself, which she attributes to her generation, why do other women treat inclusive language as a matter of great importance? This is also part of the story of a male oriented/dominated church that subordinates women to men.

It is important to note that there was a mixture of views about inclusive language across women of all ages. Language is not simply a generational matter although this is one reason why some older women are quite at ease with exclusive language. It is also a strong affirmation of the need for inclusive language today. The use of language has changed and younger generations do not understand male terms generically in the way that older generations do. This was a view expressed by a young Catholic woman: 'It's not something I would get hung up on or be terribly annoyed about or anything. I just think we have women and men in this world and it's not very difficult to change a word here and a word there to include women and men.'

However, language concerns more than changing meanings. Language is a powerful tool for both expressing and perpetuating ideas. Dale Spender has shown how language has been dominated by male thought and hence, is a means of women's continued subordination in society.[9] As Veronica Zundel states, 'If woman is "the other", the temptress, the subordinate who has to be kept safely in her place, then clearly an effective way to do so is to mention her as little as possible. And one linguistic ploy is to subsume her in the "wider" category of "mankind", so that she becomes in effect linguistically invisible.'[10] A Presbyterian woman put it this way, 'If [inclusive language] is not used it's a very subtle way of keeping women out of it, you know, almost relegating them.' An Anglican woman in her forties thought exclusive language communicated that Christianity is 'exclusively for or particular for men, or women aren't at hand, they don't come into the picture'. And for a Catholic woman in her fifties, 'language has a power to make us think in certain ways'. Therefore, language should be 'inclusive of everybody so that an injustice to women is not perpetuated, by the presupposition that everything that is "he" is acceptable and is nourishing'.

Monica Furlong comments there is great opposition to the idea of inclusive language and that this opposition has two features. On the one hand, it is regarded as too trivial and on the other, it is viewed as evil.[11] The former appears in the idea that there are 'bigger issues' to be concerned about, in the face of which, concern over inclusive language is perceived as banal, something 'really very silly', according to a Catholic woman in her twenties. One way of trivialising the concern about inclusive language is to ridicule it as an issue and make fun of those who advocate it. A Methodist woman told of how her desire for inclusive language was made fun of by the minister who 'for a while actually made jokes about me . . . I think he thought he was being funny, but he would talk about, we've got to talk about such and such for people like [and say my name].' Ridicule has been one weapon against women not simply to tease or embarrass them, but as a means of avoiding taking them seriously. 'Certain people in the congregation when we sing blatantly sexist things will look at me when I'm standing there in the choir', said a Presbyterian woman, 'and they quite often will wink at me to make me giggle, which they find amusing.'

Another manifestation of trivialisation is using inclusive language in a patronising manner that in fact undermines the whole purpose of linguistic inclusivity, that is, women's equal presence and dignity as human persons. For a Presbyterian woman this was highly offensive: 'Sometimes people will make a point "oh, we have to be politically correct nowadays so we'll . . .", you know, or situations like that where people are almost making it out as if you do have a chip on your shoulder and you have to be, you know, accommodated, as it were.'

The effect of this kind of treatment is to drain the energy of women. As one woman said of her efforts to raise the issue of inclusive language, which were met at best with misunderstanding, 'I just got worn down by it in the end, you know, and I just couldn't be annoyed, I just couldn't face the hassle.'

The other side of the opposition to inclusive language, that is, regarding it as evil, was expressed by an older Protestant woman who said, 'There are some areas like this that are dangerous that I wouldn't like to explore too much.' She went on to explain that it was 'getting into this sphere of saying that God is she and God is he and all like that'. A Methodist woman made a similar point: 'If somebody says God is female, that I would find offensive.'

As appalling as these women find the idea of inclusive language for human persons leading to inclusivity in speaking of God, it is true that inclusive language implies more than a questioning of male-oriented language for human persons. Indeed, in this respect, language is symbolic of the overall attitude and ethos of the churches towards women. It is not simply about how we speak, but who speaks and about what. As Monica Furlong argues, the strength of the opposition to inclusive language suggests that something immensely important is involved: 'exclusive language all too clearly mirrors women's centuries of invisibility and silence in the churches. Like the issue of ordaining women, a change in language indicates whether the change in church attitudes to women goes "all the way through" or is merely cosmetic. To this extent it is a political, as well as a theological matter.'[12]

While no guarantee of movement, inclusive language may be an indicator of change in institutional attitudes. For a Catholic woman in her seventies, the introduction and ownership of inclusive language in the church would 'help to bring about a change, but it's so slow that you wonder will it ever get there? . . . The one thing that there seems to be a tremendous opposition for is the thought of women priests. And I think that dominates and so the powers that be sort of feel if we give an inch at all, they'll get their foot in and before we know where we are we'll have women priests.'

'Seeing speech as a kind of action'[13] is helpful in understanding the role that language plays in silencing women and in defining humanity as either male or as female and male. Using inclusive language when speaking of human beings makes women's presence visible and challenges the idea that maleness is normative humanity from which femaleness is divergent. As a Catholic woman in her thirties said of our use of language: 'What we have to do is encapsulate the whole human experience.' Without doing so even in how we speak of one another is to further deny women full personhood within church institutions.

WOMEN STAYING NOT LEAVING

We have seen that women are not properly valued within church institutions and that they are excluded from full participation and personhood through the very structures and mind-sets that are currently inherent in these institutions. Given this analysis, let us return to the 'why stay?' question with which the book began. We do so not with the purpose of deflecting or blaming, but to listen to women's accounts of why they stay within such inhospitable institutions, why they simply do not leave. Of course, many women have left any institutional church involvement whatsoever as a way of preserving their own integrity. In doing so some, but by no means all, leave their faith behind. For the many who stay, their reasons are complex, and are reflected among the women in this book.

There are women who do not express feelings of any great struggle in their experience *as women* in their church affiliation. As one Protestant woman laughingly commented as she spoke warmly of her congregation, 'I love my church, you will get this impression!' While the majority of women expressed a desire for increased involvement by women, not all of these women aligned this view with a criticism of their institutions. Indeed, some demonstrate a certain amount of defensiveness when issues that would initiate a change in the status quo are presented, for example, the introduction of inclusive language. Among these women, some were simply unaware of issues of gender, while others held to a view that subordinated women and consequently were happy with their institutions. From some women who were more specifically critical there was also an expression of appreciation for individual leaders, clerical and lay, within their institutions who were supportive and encouraging of them in their ministries and desire for change. Other women had found ways of working within their institution (or outside of it) and in so doing found some fulfilment. Then there were those who articulated the difficulties to be faced in choosing to stay within institutions with which they had historical and faith connections and yet which they also experienced as oppressive.

How do we make sense of this range of (often overlapping) relationships to church institutions? Janet Finch's distinction between the structural position in which women are placed and women's own experience of this is helpful here. She comments that such a distinction 'enabled me to see that evidence of women successfully accommodating to various structural features of their lives in no way alters the essentially exploitative character of the structures in which they are located'.[14] Indeed, even those women who seemed unaware of or unconcerned about the male dominance and ethos of their churches, often participated at the cost of their own preferences. Women frequently commented that they would be very careful not to express their views and opinions about their church in contexts where they would be seen to be unsupportive of the leadership. This was out of deference to the individuals in such positions with their accompanying responsibilities.

Other women simply did not want to hurt another person's feelings by saying what they thought about any matter in the church and, therefore, kept silent. Such self-denial may well be the way that many women avoid conflict in the church and no doubt on occasions such reticence is valid and wise. However, as a model for community participation, it consistently means women are not present as full equal partners.

The struggle involved in staying with hostile church institutions was epitomised by a Catholic woman in her fifties: 'I still experience a powerlessness as regards the church – that I would be seen as a trouble maker. I would be seen as a feminist, which I don't see myself as, someone that creates hassle. And that if I did want to do something and I needed the priests' permission, that I would find that they weren't willing if I was critical, and I suppose that would be the sense of powerlessness that I have. For instance, when I go to mass on Sunday I feel so angry about the non-inclusive language that's used I spend my time at mass writing letters. But I never get round to sending them and I come out so angry and there's part of me that says it doesn't matter whether you write or not, they're not going to change. So there is that powerlessness . . . There's a lot going on within me about that whole aspect of women in the church and the non-inclusive language and I come out from mass and I say, I'm that much away, that tiny bit away from leaving all of this. And I think I will be like I am with my own family that, though I am in pain at times with them, I will hang in there because leaving them I would have such a sense of isolation that it would be worst than the first state.'

Identity, belonging and community are all part of women's connection to churches. Hence, for a Methodist woman, 'to a certain extent the church is something about coming home'. This does not remove the difficulties of belonging, which are variously negotiated. For some women it is their recognition of the fallibility of the church as a human institution which could be distinguished from God that enabled them to remain within it. 'I learnt to separate church and God, they're two different things', said one young woman who, in making a 'conscious decision' to be part of it, focused on the good things in her church. A Catholic woman in her forties commented how she had 'been brought up . . . within this whole thing that the church was right, always right, no matter what happened, and I started realising that that is not true. I mean the church here isn't God.' It was this realisation that enabled her to return to the life of the church rather than being estranged from it.

This idea of autonomy was spoken of frequently by the women interviewed. Autonomy is about women taking responsibility for themselves, which does not preclude responsibility and accountability to others. As Daphne Hampson comments, 'To be "autonomous" is to let one's own law rule one: literally in Greek to be *autonomos* (self-law). The word, etymologically, does not mean independence. It need not imply conceiving of oneself as an isolated atom in competition with others. Indeed, that it has come to hold such connotations may tell us much about the male psyche within patriarchy; as though the only way to be oneself, to take responsibility for oneself, were to set oneself up over against others.'[15] As a Catholic woman in her thirties put it, 'I take permission myself, I don't ask for it.' A woman in her seventies said, 'I know that I kick myself at times, I don't get angry, but I think what a waste of time. I've been listening to men all the time and I knew what God was saying to me and the men hadn't a clue.'

For a number of women, not waiting for permission in conjunction with the frustration of lack of opportunity within denominations meant they 'had to go outside, I had to go outside to do lots of things'. Consequently, 'the church to me is missing out on those gifts'. A few women spoke of choosing which congregations in which to worship depending on the cleric officiating in order to avoid experiencing exclusive liturgies. Others focused less on the institution itself and more on relationships either within or outside of their congregations. So, rather than viewing the services as vitally important, one woman spoke of seeing 'growth through the relationships much, much more important . . . being challenged and growing and maturing as being much more important'.

Some women expressed fatigue at battling with the institutions and, therefore, were less active within them. 'I think I spent a lot of years believing in the maxim of changing the church from within and I suppose I kind of don't care about that anymore. Somebody else can change it from within', a Catholic woman said wearily. 'And I do believe it's possible to change from within but you go so, so slowly and I mean you kind of get fed up being in groups where you're the most extreme person in it.' Another woman agrees: 'I get irritated at the structures and just the whole hierarchy and the masculine approach to everything . . . I would like to be involved but I don't want to be involved in current structures and I don't know if I want to get involved in changing something else . . . I suppose I've got fed up with being knocked.'

Against this background it is not surprising that, in their commitment and desire for a faith community, there are those who stay within church institutions by letting go of their dreams for full inclusion. As noted in chapter one, one Anglican woman told how she had deliberately let a lot of issues around women in the church go because most feminists that she knew ended up outside of the church institutions and she did not want to. This left her in a position where 'I don't have anybody who thinks like me who I can worship with. Now I don't know whether that's just because I haven't really gone looking, but in the Anglican church there isn't anyone who I really know who is where I'm at. And I sort of feel that I haven't moved very much in the last while because nobody is stimulating me to move.'

Women's connection and involvement with church institutions involves relationship, belonging and community. After all, 'it has been the bearer of the story of Jesus Christ and the good news of God's love'.[16] This, of course, is why it is so painful to experience exclusion in churches and also why so many women do not want to leave.

When two or three gather . . .

To engage church institutions in addressing their exclusionary practice and ethos does not at the outset determine the outcome of facing a feminist critique. The task is, in the words of Letty Russell, to 'sit back and ask ourselves about what is happening among us when two or three gather in Christ's name and begin to think through possible ways of being church that will affirm the full humanity of *all* women and men'.[17] Imagining the church as such a place is important. Letty Russell, for example, uses the symbol of a table around which people gather and experience the welcome of others to describe her 'vision of Christian community of faith and struggle that practices God's hospitality'.[18] This concept of 'church in the round' contrasts to hierarchical models of church which marginalise women (and others). Indeed, the 'ultimate goal of God's household is to do away with the margin and the centre by joining the one who is at the centre of life in the church but dwells on the margin where he lived and died'.[19]

Rosemary Radford Ruether envisions the church as a community for people liberated from sexism for sexism is 'a serious expression of human sinfulness, of alienation from authentic existence'.[20] She understands clericalism by definition to be about having power over others rather than empowering others: 'The basic assumption of clericalism is that the people have no direct access to the divine.'[21] Hence, she sees the necessity for clericalism to be dismantled in favour of a model of ministry seen as mutual empowerment based on individual gifting. While this dismantling may be done by a 'clergy-led revolutionizing of a local church'[22] in which an understanding of the church as a liberation community becomes central, the difficulty is that clergy are seldom willing to relinquish their clerical prerogatives and share power with the laity. This sense of preserving clericalism is the reason Anne Thurston suggests that ultimately it may be that within the Catholic Church it is those who are most anxious to maintain the hierarchical status who, in the absence of male clerical candidates, will advocate the ordination of women. Therefore, she too is concerned first of all to enquire what kind of church we actually want. She suggests the key question becomes whether equality in ministry and ministry practised as service to the Christian community is enabled or impeded by present structures.[23]

One way of exploring alternative modes of being church is in autonomous feminist groups or base communities which take responsibility 'for reflecting on, celebrating, and acting on the understanding of redemption as liberation from patriarchy'.[24] This is not a model of isolation from or 'sectarian rejection'[25] of institutional churches, but the means to have creative dialogue between the two, while those initiating the feminist challenge to the status quo are nurtured in a supportive community. Indeed, Letty Russell claims that such nurturing base communities are one reason why many feminist women remain within established church institutions; the experience of integrating their worship and life in these new communities enables them to maintain their relationship to and activity within existing church institutions. She also comments that the church as the people of God is something that belongs to all Christians, many of whom refuse to be squeezed out of the community. Further, feminist struggle with church institutions is in keeping with the gospel narratives which depict Jesus as confronting unjust religious practices which he encountered.[26]

Addressing women's subordination within church institutions is an arduous task. The path is difficult and consumes energy when emerging from a supportive community base; to pursue this route as an isolated individual without the support and nurture of like-minded others as was the case with a number of those interviewed, is perhaps rarely possible. In such instances, withdrawing from the struggle is a means of survival for individual women.

The experience of women who stay within institutions and find a way to witness to an alternative way of being Christian community has been described as 'defecting in place'.[27] For Rosemary Radford Ruether 'it is the option of the "defectors in place" that is both more creative and more authentic than that of the polarizers of either right or left, for they remain faithful to a dialectical, transformative process and affirm both the good elements and also ambiguity in all our human traditions. But in order to sustain their both-and option, they will have to become much more mature in their understanding of this option, much more able to face their accusers of both right and left without fear or guilt and to give reasons for rejecting their mutually exclusive alternatives.'[28]

Such creativity and courage is necessary if church institutions are to give practical embodiment to a theology of women's full personhood.

Chapter 6

THE 'IN-THE-MIDDLE' GOD:
Women, community conflict and power

Women feel more powerless . . . and I think that translates itself into women's perception on whether it is possible for them to influence societal events.

Catholic woman in her forties

Civil conflict with its social, cultural, political, religious and economic aspects, has been part of the pervasive backcloth against which women in Northern Ireland conduct their lives. While the troubles[1] themselves are specific to Northern Ireland, some of the inherent dynamics that impede women's development here can be found in other situations of civil strife. In this chapter we look at how different forms of oppression are interwoven together and why women's empowerment in their community is important to overcome their subordination. In this exploration a picture of God emerges which fosters women's empowerment, enabling them to engage on behalf of themselves and others in the society in which they live.

MULTIPLE OPPRESSION

Northern Ireland has become synonymous with the sectarian[2] conflict of the troubles. The violence and awfulness of this civil unrest with its thirty plus years of accumulated memory and experience is imprinted on all aspects of life in Northern Ireland. This is true not only for those whose painful encounters with the more brutal manifestations of the conflict have left deep marks on their lives. It also applies to those who, by virtue of their social and geographical location, appear to have been left relatively untouched by the more obvious elements of community divisions. As a Methodist woman encapsulated: 'The troubles have done more than just the killings, it's the whole culture.' The dominance of the sectarian conflict, however, has obscured the existence of other conflicts, including the sexism that perpetuates a secondary position for women.

The invisibility of women's lives in Northern Ireland is, in part, due to the priority given to the national question. All other things have been seen as secondary to resolving the constitutional issue as to which political jurisdiction Northern Ireland belongs: the United Kingdom or the Republic of Ireland. Key to the 1998 Belfast Agreement was the provision of a democratic framework to resolve this matter.[3] At the time this gathered cross-community as well as Republican and Loyalist paramilitary support. However, insecurities and deeply held convictions about nationality continue to impede the progress that the Agreement potentially offers.

In practice, seeing women's status and participation as secondary to other concerns not only postpones, belittles, or refuses to acknowledge women's reality. It also suggests that issues of gender are irrelevant to the national question. In doing this, it overlooks the interlocking nature of oppressions that may be at work in a society. The women in this book spoke of the interweaving of three forms of injustice – class, race and sex – with the sectarian conflict in Northern Ireland.

Addressing their subordination means paying attention to each of these components.

It is not simply that there are a number of injustices such as class inequalities, sexism,[4] racism and sectarianism, in operation. Rather these prejudices and discriminations interplay to enforce and multiply injustices. 'I would say the Catholic upbringing didn't do too much for self-confidence', reflected a woman in her forties. 'It wasn't the only thing. I mean, growing up where I did in [a predominantly Protestant rural town] – we were a large Catholic family, we also were poor . . . you kind of kept your head down, you tended to do the same in the church as well . . . [you felt] second-class.' For this woman, minority community status and economic inequalities are linked with a sense of religious inferiority and poor self-image. As a result, while she identified herself as Catholic, she commented that 'one of the legacies of my childhood is that . . . I certainly avoid going around revealing to people that I'm a Catholic or that I'm from a Catholic background'.

Another woman spoke of racism she and her family had encountered from her church, society and paramilitaries. Her church congregation had excluded her from an important element of its community life on spurious grounds and which she had no doubt was due to race issues. Commenting on this institutional church experience she said: 'there was that cold feeling about the church at that time . . . I could still cry' and she became tearful. Her family had also been subject to explicit racism from churchgoers (outside of the institutional church context), which had caused them considerable disruption. In addition, paramilitaries had repeatedly attacked family property and influenced other people on how to behave towards them. The fact that her family voted in support of the constitutional stance to which the paramilitary group adhered was not considered. 'But what can you do?' she asked. 'You can just say, "Father forgive them", because you understand they are in darkness spiritually, aren't they? I couldn't have got through without God. I couldn't have survived those things. I would have been in a mental hospital or whatever.' These experiences have left this woman with a profound sense of alienation: 'You can't trust anybody because people do things in the belief that they're right and that they are doing the right thing, don't you think? And I'm sure I misinterpret people's motives often.'[5]

The single issue focus on sectarian conflict hides the racism that is increasingly apparent in Northern Ireland society and which is not unrelated to the Unionist/Nationalist struggle for equality and identity. For the discrimination and violence that is part of sectarianism is transferred to any who are perceived as being outside the identity boundary of the perpetrators of that discrimination or violence. In this way they exercise dominance, thereby bolstering their own identity.

This interlocking nature of oppressive ideology and practice is seen also in the patriarchal agendas evident in sectarianism. A woman who had been terrifyingly intimidated by paramilitaries had been told that this intimidation was directly linked to the content of her work with women from the other side of the community division who 'were beginning to do a lot more studying around . . . this whole thing that they can't say no within a marriage – sex and things like that. And the fact that they aren't just here to have children and there's other alternatives and other ways of looking at things and thinking about things. And marriage being a partnership rather than a dominant partner. And that whole query about self-assertiveness within women . . . I found that quite funny because I knew it was very strong in [my] faith, you know, the dominant male thing, but that was my first real experience of it being very, very strong within [their] faith.' As a result, 'the men weren't just having it all their own way, you know. And some of them weren't particularly liking this.'

This is not only a story about sectarian oppression. It is also the story of men intimidating one woman in order to maintain dominance over other women. Yet it is not two distinct stories, but a tale of two injustices woven together into an oppressive whole. Without denying the very real differences among women with divergent national aspirations, any resolution of the national question cannot in and of itself challenge the subordination of women, both Nationalist and Unionist, while gender inequalities are not addressed.[6]

So, it is not simply that sexism, classism and racism are three other issues that need to be dealt with in a situation of sectarian conflict when priorities allow. Rather, sexism, classism, racism and sectarianism are all part of a mind-set and set of systems and structures whereby, for whatever reason, a group with one identity think, act and exert power in prejudicial and harmful ways towards another group. And in any society these work together not in terms of additions of oppression and discrimination, but their interaction produces a multiplication of effect and consequence.

In order to overcome women's inequality we need to pay attention to all forms of discrimination in which all women are subordinate in some manner, but some women also know advantage. Any system that privileges some women over others is ultimately detrimental to all women. This is because such a system is based on a model of domination/subordination and it is this model itself that seeks expression in the context of difference, be it of economic status, dis/ability, race, gender or community affiliation.

POWERLESSNESS AND EMPOWERMENT

How do women begin to address their secondary status in a situation of community division? The women in this book have a range of experiences and attitudes in respect of the troubles.[7] There are those who, either personally or through their family or close friends, have been involved in bomb explosions, shooting incidents and arson attacks; experienced verbal assault and physical injury; known employment discrimination; received intimidation or death threats; and witnessed death and bereavement (including several women who spoke of their work in hospitals that had brought them into close contact with the physical and emotional aftermath of violent incidents).

Some women were actively endeavouring to address sectarianism. 'I wouldn't be in the job I'm doing now if it hadn't been for the troubles', said a community sector worker. 'I've always had a thing about trying to change, trying to do something, as an individual responsibility, do something rather than hide . . . [What] bothers me in sectarianism [is] the hate and so I would want to do something about it rather than be passive.' Others, however, felt like they co-existed with the situation. 'I feel affected because of [where I lived]', a Presbyterian woman in her forties explained, 'but in many ways I've kept my head down, it's been a matter of tolerating it and getting on, that attitude, you know, keeping it in the background and just getting on with life. I've detached myself from it all at the same time living through it. A number of my neighbours were murdered, I've been in shooting incidences and murder incidences so it has impacted quite a bit and yet in another way it hasn't.'

For some there was a sense of feeling physically or emotionally removed from the community conflict. 'I can be objective about it', commented a Catholic woman in her seventies. 'I would tune into the world service and the BBC and listen in to all the things that are happening around the world, you know, and they would be just as equally oppressive and upsetting as what is happening here.' She had found living in an area with Nationalist and Republican graffiti 'very difficult . . . and I just couldn't belong to that kind of a situation'. A Presbyterian woman over fifty stated: 'Fortunately the troubles have not had much impact on our lives in that, you know, we haven't had any close family relations killed or injured or anything like that. We know people who were bereaved, but it hasn't touched on us really.'

The idea that the troubles 'hasn't touched us really' refers to not being direct victims of violence or injustice, the more overt hallmarks of the conflict. However, the reality of living in a divided society is reflected in the way that issues of national or religious identities and loyalties dominate social relations. Speaking of her time as a nursing student, a Protestant woman commented how she and her roommates automatically introduced themselves to each other in terms of their names, hometown and religion. A Catholic woman expressed how pervasive such identification is: 'It is intrinsic in all of us [that] no matter whether you intellectually want to or not, if you've grown up in Northern Ireland it is second nature to you to suss out someone's religion . . . It's not necessarily for any ulterior motive. It's just . . . indigenous to growing up here.'

Such categorisation is accompanied by expectations of behaviour that support and sustain particular identities. 'I was expected to be very Republican, Nationalist,' said a Catholic woman referring to the views of other Catholic people, 'and I wasn't prepared to go into that mould . . . [They] expected me to be very Irish, in the narrow sense of being Irish . . . There was a strange sense in which Northern Irish Catholics maybe expected me to be elevating the Irish language and everything Irish and I never felt any need to do that . . . I love the Irish language . . . but not in a triumphalist way.' She spoke of her experience in a cross-community prayer group when a Catholic member said to her, 'Oh, I thought you were Protestant.' This 'was a very subtle way of saying you do Protestant things, you know. And that was because I wouldn't fall into the stereotype, you know, of what was expected of Catholics in the Catholic group.' A Methodist woman protested about experiencing a similar dynamic. 'I hate people put into boxes', she stated emphatically, 'I don't want to be put into a box, I want to be myself . . . I don't want people thinking she's a Protestant, so she must vote this way or be this way or think this way.'

Such attitudes, reflecting the systemic sectarianism[8] in operation, have an imprisoning effect that is oppressive. Two women who had both spent time outside of Northern Ireland were very aware of this. 'One of the main reasons that I didn't want to come back was I did not want to come back to the climate of fear and suspicion', explained a Catholic woman. 'I did not want to come back to the parochiality of attitudes that I had left behind when I left here. I didn't want to come back to getting searched going into shops and pubs. I didn't want to come back to army on the streets. I didn't want to come back to the bitterness and bigotry and the segregation that there was between Catholics and Protestants. I just didn't want it.'[9] For an Anglican woman, 'Most of the time, I have to be honest, it just goes on and I just think, is it ever going to stop? It's just a bit of the background. But every time I go away and come back it's just so suffocating. I just feel so oppressed and I feel why can't it just stop, please end it. I go through periods of intense praying about it and asking for peace and what can I do and then other times it just goes on.'

The last woman's fluctuating relationship to the situation from intensity to 'it just goes on' reflects a sense of powerlessness among some women in the way they relate to the situation of community conflict. This powerlessness is a sense of women feeling unable to change or alter their situation on either a personal or community level. Sometimes this is expressed in terms of frustration, confusion, pain or helplessness. After a particularly difficult time of community tension and aggression around marching disputes, one woman said, 'it put me as a Catholic woman on the ground with people walking on me' and she spoke of feeling 'like there was no hope'.

Some women expressed a sense of disempowerment through lack of political or cultural identity. 'I don't think I have a culture,' a Methodist woman stated, 'I think the troubles have taken that away.' A Presbyterian woman spoke of having 'always tried to err on the side of being open and accepting other people's attitudes, but having said that I do feel I haven't really embraced my political or even a cultural heritage. I've tried to keep in no man's land, which isn't really the thing to do either. I can't get motivated emotionally in a political way.' One woman spoke of how she had 'closed off from [the troubles] a long time ago' and hence, 'wouldn't dream of being involved in politics'.

While not the story of every woman in Northern Ireland, this common feeling of powerlessness contrasts with the notion of empowerment, which is 'the process by which individuals, families, groups, and communities increase their personal, interpersonal, socioeconomic, and political strength and influence in order to improve their well-being. Empowerment is not granted from an external source but emerges from within as persons and communities acknowledge and appreciate their gifts and their responsibilities.'[10] Clearly, this is different from an understanding of power as something a person or group of people exercise over others. Rather, empowerment is experienced by individuals or groups as they assume responsibility for themselves. While this does not mean that they can completely control their social environment, it does mean that they become active agents in their situation, seeking to address it in whatever form is appropriate for constructive purposes.

An example of this comes from a Catholic woman who spoke of how she had joined the Alliance Party,[11] which was 'very hard for me to do', but which was a response to the powerlessness she felt at the time in the face of discrimination and sectarianism: 'That was my only way – how could [you] with all this going on, what could you do? You were powerless and they [the Alliance Party] came along and that was an opening for working with Protestants and Catholics together.'

One woman attributed her alienation from political involvement to a sense of powerlessness which was forged not only as a result of growing up as part of a minority community, but also to her experience as a woman. It 'has something to do with being a woman as well. I mean, research would indicate that women feel more powerless because they see that things are more personal. I mean . . . research [into] promotion [shows] women invariably thought that they had been promoted because they had been in the right place at the right time whereas men . . . [it was more] that you were the best person for the job. And I think that translates itself into women's perception on whether it is possible for them to influence societal events.'

There are a number of interrelated reasons for women's feelings of powerlessness or empowerment in respect of community conflict. Individual personal biographies, of course, affect women's attitudes and actions. A woman whose husband's life had been threatened had lived for many years with the fear that 'at the back of my mind I was aware that I could become a widow'. She had conducted her life taking this into account, ensuring work for herself that energised her and which she loved. Yet she did not shirk from doing what she felt was right in regard to community issues, 'we . . . can justify our actions, you know, nothing we have done we would regret'. Against this background she also was reticent about expressing herself: 'I sort of keep things under my belt and you don't see . . . the whole of me, that's just me, I can't explain that. There's a certain reserve within me that will not speak out about my inner most feelings. So when it comes to the troubles, I'll not speak out about my inner most feelings and certainly not to those who would oppose me.'

The alienation from political involvement in Northern Ireland is in no small part due to its male dominated public and political culture.[12] Unfortunately, there is a cycle perpetuated by women's exclusion from mainstream political activity in that 'women are ignored because they are assumed to be powerless and, being ignored, they may be affirmed in their sense of powerlessness'.[13] A complicating factor in Northern Ireland is that the 'national question' has played a divisive role in women's political activism.[14] In the 1970s and 80s women were able to form alliances to work on various socio-economic issues of mutual concern and in doing so made a significant impact for local communities, in welfare provision and on legislation.[15] However, their ability to address political structures and constitutional issues was largely hindered by competing loyalties arising out of the conflict.

The current phase of the peace process (from 1996 onwards) has given women greater visibility within the public sphere in Northern Ireland, partly through the involvement of the Northern Ireland Women's Coalition (NIWC). The NIWC is a non-sectarian, broad-based coalition of women of all political hues and religions, made up of academics, trade union activists, and voluntary sector and community workers. It was formed just six weeks prior to the May 1996 elections for the Northern Ireland Forum for Political Dialogue, to ensure that women's voices would be included in the political process.[16]

Increased political participation does give women a sense of empowerment. However, as Elisabeth Porter comments, many women 'are still learning the skills of empowerment'.[17] In reviewing studies of women's activism in Northern Ireland, she notes that while those with political and trade union experience have known a sense of empowerment, 'we cannot assume that all women have developed their capacities likewise'.[18] There is, therefore, a need to concentrate on developing women's capabilities. For the women involved in the NIWC, acquiring political skills was very much part of their participation in the public world: 'The bottom line was that the NIWC was a political education project on a huge scale.'[19]

That said, women's growing empowerment in political matters meets additional hurdles because women are assigned to the private sphere. 'Empowered women become tired of the stresses involved in combining the triple load of paid work, domestic labour and child-rearing with always having to fight against patriarchal values and structures.'[20] In addition, the context of community conflict further exacerbates this situation, for there seems to be a link between internal conflict and heightened traditionalism in the role of women. 'It is a curious paradox that conflict, however much it may be outwardly directed towards bringing about change in society, can be at the same time an inherently conservative agent. The sense of insecurity that accompanies such disturbances reflects strongly upon women, particularly where they are represented as the custodians of a society's cultural values . . . Thus we may find . . . a tension existing between women who find new opportunities to express themselves politically and men who step up their efforts and control women and try to reinforce the boundary that separates the domestic from the public sphere.'[21] Certainly in Northern Ireland the women's movement has been concerned with matters aimed at supporting family life without a robust challenge to traditional gender divisions. Hence, the term 'family feminist' describes the nature of many women's activism.[22]

The sense of powerlessness that exists among some women is not unrelated to their exclusion from the so-called public world and their restriction to the private sphere (as explored in chapter three). Women need to find a sense of ownership of the public world of politics, which itself needs transforming in order to value equally and fully women's contributions and participation in order to ensure that women's activities enhance their well-being.

Lack of empowerment, be it political, cultural or social, is a form of psychological disenfranchisement. What part can faith play in the empowerment of Christian women?

THE 'IN-THE-MIDDLE' GOD

'I suppose really when it comes down to it we've had to trust the Lord a lot, lot more in this situation than what we would have to do in many's another situation.' These words of a Presbyterian woman are an expression of trust in God in a context of conflict in which personal vulnerability is exposed. A Catholic woman spoke of 'a tremendous level of dependence on God because you had to sort of say, well I'm going to have to go out and just get on with this, you know . . . recognise the fear is there and try to work with it'.

It is not that trusting God for these women is simply an acknowledgement of their own powerlessness and hence, a sense of their own empowerment would make their faith redundant. Dependence upon God is assumed in the understanding of God as loving creator from whom humanity receives the possibility of existence and well-being. Situations that expose human vulnerabilities bring this aspect of the relationship to God into sharper focus. Faith is a complex interweaving of life experience, personal commitment, belief and practice, and involvement with a community of believers. The trauma of life in a violent, divided society (as with other life experiences and situations) subjects faith to critical questioning. Speaking of the sectarian murder of her friends an Anglican woman explained, 'I sort of thought, well God why didn't you stop them, but again I sort of feel that God allows us to do our own thing. I find that a bit hard to accept at times. You know, I think why doesn't he interfere and get involved? So, you know, the troubles have made me question an awful lot.' A Catholic woman reflected on her personal experience of the trauma of her family being caught up in a bomb explosion: 'I don't believe that God would want anybody to be taken in a bomb, but I think God can change a bad situation and bring good out of it. That's different to saying it's God's will . . . I don't think half of the things that are said to be God's will are God's will.'

Trusting in God for each of the above four women is a matter of personal faith and integrity. It does not preclude active involvement in facing the community division in Northern Ireland. Each of these women is engaged in addressing sectarianism in their respective situations. However, for other women, trust in God, when combined with a lack of personal or communal agency, finds expression in a dependence on God's actions to the exclusion of their own. 'A lot of people say, where is God in the midst of all this? And I think you can't help asking that sometimes,' said a woman in her sixties. 'My faith tells me that he is there and he's in control, but it's just very difficult to understand sometimes why it's all been let happen.' A Methodist woman echoes a similar thought: 'The troubles don't bother me because I have the theory that God is working through them. I don't mean that I'm not sad when there's a tragedy. I feel very much for people . . . who suffer. But I've accepted that God is working.'

In contrast, for a Presbyterian woman, Christian faith implicated her in her social surroundings: 'I suppose living here if the troubles haven't had an effect on our Christian faith – I suppose I should talk about myself – if the troubles hadn't had an effect on *my* Christian faith, I would feel it would say something about my faith, you know. Because we can't live in and around violence and hatred . . . without taking account of it and without making it part of – we can't just say well that's just ten per cent of the population and that's nothing to do with us.' An Anglican woman put it succinctly, '[If] the gospel isn't relating to Northern Ireland then what are we at here?' A Catholic woman explained that for her this meant 'that I was going to try do something. So I became known . . . as the liberal one that would go to all the Protestant services. And that I would try and cross the divide and all that . . . try and break down the barriers and let each other see that the horns the other person has aren't real horns at all, you know, it's just because of what we're carrying from our background and it's so silly carrying all this . . . I just had a calling to have a deep relationship with God and this all just came out of it, you know. And once you start having a relationship you have to start opening out to everybody.'

Each of these three women illustrates what we looked at in chapter two, namely the connection between human life experiences and concepts of God. While the focus in that chapter was on sex/gender identity, the various experiences of women in the troubles also demonstrate this connection. It is not that *any* understanding of God is valid simply because it is related to a life experience. Rather, individual experience dialogues with Christian tradition and faith communities to illuminate our understanding of God. Engagement with the difficulties of life in a divided society reveals an understanding of God as caught up in the trauma of human reality rather than detached from it: 'I've had so much, because of working in [a hospital in Belfast] in the early seventies, you know, terrible pain just. You know, I can remember going on duty as a very junior student nurse to work in theatre or recovery ward or something and there had been some atrocity during the night and you'd have all these bags sitting at theatre door and these were all the limbs of people that had been blown up during the night. And sort of going in and seeing all these people, you know, just innocent victims, if you like, people just going about doing their own thing and just caught up in things. And I sort of felt an overwhelming sort of grief, you know, and felt that it was all so, you know, just wasted and feeling, you know, how much more must God feel that, you know, because we'd been given so much and yet we do this to each other.'

A dualistic world view that separates spirit and matter has kept God apart from the ordinary, earthly, everyday matters of life. As we have seen, this has disastrous consequences for women in particular who in dualistic thought have been associated with that which is physical, natural, material and hence, have been seen as corrupting influences and kept away from that which is seen as holy. In so far as dualism perpetuates an understanding of God and all associated with the divine as needing to be kept separate and above material realities, it provides no model or incentive for Christians to engage in the risky and difficult business of resolving community conflict.

In contrast to the idea of God as removed and above human concerns, one woman, out of her own experience of conflict, understands God to be in the most difficult of places, namely, in the middle of conflict: 'God is able to be in the middle of situations of total opposites and not be crushed by them. The difference between God and us is that when we get stuck in the middle we get pulled apart and, for me, you have to choose sides because it's too painful to be on two sides at once.

Whereas God can stay in the middle and survive. I suppose for me God is love but what it means is . . . for me it became clearest when somebody I knew was very, very badly [injured] . . . and I was working with people who belonged to the organisation who did that . . . Or another [example] would be where you're working with two partners . . . two people in love who are trying to go in different directions, and . . . there came a point where I realised that to stay sane I could only work on one side, I would choose one side. I think I chose generally . . . the side without power. But that was in order to stay [sane] because to stay there in the middle was such a crucifying experience that there was no way you could live there, it was too painful. For me that was the difference that God can actually be there in the middle and fully feel and everything else, the different sides, and still stay there. To me that was the difference I suppose between God and us.'

To listen to more of this last woman's story is to understand that actually she is staying 'in the middle' in a number of courageous ways as part of her daily life. The picture she and others provide is of God immersed in the pain of human conflict rather than removed from it. An Anglican woman spoke of the bigotry she had been subject to because she was married to a Catholic. Experiencing the vulnerability of her own situation she reflected, 'I suppose the fact that Jesus was vulnerable, you know, I think it has made me understand more how much he did, if you like, what the cost was. The fact that he, I mean nobody was more abused than he was, and he didn't have to do it. And I think experiencing [vulnerability] a bit ourselves, I think I feel the pain of the divisions here very, very strongly and, again, I think that must be what God feels like.'

Both of these women are developing the idea of incarnation, of 'God with us', in the context of the many manifestations of community conflict. An incarnational theology provides these women with a model of God being with them in their difficulties and in their endeavours to work in situations of conflict. Hence, empowerment is not a smooth continuum of increasing ease of being. It does not preclude suffering or anguish.

To advocate women's empowerment through political or social means or through their understanding of God (all of which are spiritual endeavours) is not to prescribe the nature that such involvement should have. The task of accommodating genuine differences within community traditions and experiences (including their religious enmeshment) and seeking political and socio-religious resolution is a different subject.[23] The point here is that part of women's empowerment involves taking some ownership of the social and political spaces in Northern Ireland that deal with community issues. In doing this, women enter public spaces from which they have largely been excluded in the past. This exclusion has meant their minimal access to public and political power structures which have mitigated against them and their concerns. For Christian women, a theology that endorses the value of human existence and understands God as immanent as well as transcendent to the realities of Northern Ireland's particularity is part of a faith that energises them to deal with conflict. Their involvement may be on any number of levels. Several women referred to their contributions in the diminutive. A Methodist woman living in a particularly volatile area, talking of her desire to cross the boundaries to Catholic people in that region, said 'I feel a tremendous responsibility to pray about . . . the troubles. And . . . I would love to have a role in being a bridge and there is no big bridge open to me at the moment or obvious – there are lots of little ones and I jump at every opportunity and have done since 1969.' Feminism has always valued the small, seemingly inconsequential things of life because it has valued the women whose time and energy has been involved in everyday ordinariness. To do something rather than nothing was expressed by a Catholic woman in her sixties, 'God was asking me to do this. There was some drive in me asking me to do this. I wouldn't have been aware of it say in the beginning but when I'm looking back on it I can see that God was choosing somebody to try and, you know, do their wee bit, not much but I mean that wee bit was given you to do.' While this woman describes her engagement as a 'wee bit', it was actually both courageous and at the time prophetic.[24]

An incarnational theology that views God as involved in all human affairs provides people of faith with an impetus to be involved regardless of personal experience of violence or injustice.[25] One woman spoke of how coming from an environment where she had never experienced overt discrimination or sectarian violence, she moved to an interface area. There she became 'involved in the life of the people and saw things and heard things that really were very foreign to me, but I took on board and again I tried to make sense of for the people. And that was very often kind of going against my own middle-class background, you know, and my own image of church and my own concept of right and wrong, you know. I think that was one of the graces of God really that I held myself open to new things and tried not to be judgemental.'

For Christian women, a theology that overturns a dualistic understanding of the relationship of God to human reality and which provides women with a sense of personal agency is required to enable them to actively involve themselves in whatever way they can in a divided society. The identity of 'God-with-us' and 'in-the-middle' of conflicting situations is both commitment and companionship and hence, part of women's empowerment.

Chapter 7

WELL-WOMAN CHRISTIANITY: *Epilogue*

Jesus said to the woman, 'Your faith has saved you; go in peace.'
Luke 7:50

Jesus said to her, 'Daughter, your faith has made you well; go in peace.'
Luke 8:48

How does faith go from being something that saves and gives well-being, to something that diminishes women's humanity? We have seen how women's subordination has roots in dualistic thought which places women in an oppositional relationship to men and masculinist values. In particular, in Christianity it is endorsed through a God – man – woman hierarchy in which women are not only assigned an inferior position to men, but also given a negative identity in regard to the divine and consequently normative humanity. While not always articulated in this manner, this thought pattern outworks itself in terms of the way we speak of God, think of ourselves, order our faith communities, and organise our social relations.

What we need is a transformed vision of theological and

social reality in which models of dominance and subjection are replaced by structures, ideologies and ways of relating that value women (and men) in all their diversity. What we have is various theological and cultural mechanisms combining together to undermine the full and equal humanity of Christian women. The importance of understanding the nature of these mechanisms is that frequently they operate unexamined and hence remain undisturbed by other changes regarding women.

Think, for example, of what happens if we do not have an understanding of the divinely endorsed dualistic construction of gender within Christianity. We may incorporate female metaphors when speaking of God, laud women's caring natures, and give women access to ordination and government in some church institutions, but this does not sufficiently challenge women's subordinate status. Indeed, it may actually perpetuate it, albeit in modern form, because the changes that do occur give the appearance of women's equality and inclusion while leaving largely untouched the framework that maintains women's secondary and marginal status. So, female images of God are used only occasionally and limited to so-called feminine aspects of God. They are not used habitually as gender equivalent images thereby counteracting the association of maleness with deity. Women's practice of care is given recognition but, reinforced by a gendered application of Christian self-denial, it continues to be exploited by structural inequalities. It is not affirmed as part of what it means to be human with its proper value reflected in social arrangements. Women are permitted to become part of institutional church government yet not necessarily with any encouragement. Nor are the structures of government reviewed to mirror the consequences of women's inclusion.

It is not that changes such as these are not important. However, a commitment to address women's reality within Christianity will involve a rigorous examination of the nature of women's subordination. Without such investment of time, energy, will and passion, Christian women will remain in a position which restricts their humanity as those made in the image of God.

Is such feminist engagement with Christian faith a way to 'go in peace'? Will it not, in fact, uncomfortably disturb the composure of our Christian communities? Well, yes, but this equanimity has been achieved at women's expense. For when we examine the mechanisms of women's continued subordination we are exposing an injustice that currently exists, not creating a situation of conflict that could have been avoided. Often it is those women who, intentionally or not, draw attention to women's situation (sometimes simply by their presence and other times by their activity) who face accusations (either from others or within themselves) of being disruptive, disloyal, overly sensitive, silly, dysfunctional or disobedient. This places the responsibility for any disharmony within Christianity that results from women's presence or action on women themselves. A fuller understanding of the relationships of dominance and subjection, however, makes clear that the so-called 'women's issue' involves everyone owning a Christian identity. This is because an alternative vision of the full and equal humanity of Christian women concerns a partnership of mutuality between women and men in which the difference of sex is not used to create a hierarchy of men over women. Rarely even attempted, this alternative way of relating remains difficult to envisage in all its possibilities.

It would, however, be one in which the orthodox notion that God is neither male nor female becomes embodied in Christian teaching, practice and institutional church life. One where structural and ideological changes would foster the potential for women and men to more fully actualise a Christian understanding of humanity made in the image of God. In other words, a view of human personhood that places equal worth and value on women as autonomous selves-in-relation, and which is implemented in personal, social and ecclesiological structures and relationships.

When we pay attention to the mechanisms that perpetuate women's subordination we make visible women's reality. In doing so we offer ourselves the possibility of working towards a gender inclusive Christian understanding, one which ensures that women's choice of the 'better part' will not be taken away.

NOTES

1: WOMEN'S WORLD

1. Luke 10:9. The kingdom of God is neither geographical realm nor political reign, but concerns the liberation of God in people's lives (Luke 4:18–19). It is essentially relational – the justice of right relations with God, with each other and in society and, hence, has personal and political implications.
2. Ann Loades (ed.), 1990, *Feminist Theology: A Reader*, London: SPCK, p. 2.
3. Mary Stewart van Leeuwen (ed.), 1993, *After Eden: Facing The Challenge of Gender Reconciliation*, Grand Rapids: Eerdmans, p. 121.
4. Rosemary Radford Ruether, 1996, 'Patriarchy' in Lisa Isherwood and Dorothea McEwan (eds), *An A to Z of Feminist Theology*, Sheffield: Sheffield Academic Press, pp. 173–174, p. 174.
5. ibid.
6. Serene Jones, 2000, *Feminist Theory and Christian Theology: Cartographies of Grace*, Minneapolis: Fortress Press, p. 71.
7. I focus on feminist standpoint theory rather than other feminist (for example, essentialist or postmodern) theoretical use of women's experience because of the former's emphasis on understanding women's reality from their experiences of oppression and hence, its advocacy for social, political (and indeed religious) transformation.
8. Nancy Hartsock, 1987, 'The Feminist Standpoint: Developing the Ground for a Specifically Feminist Historical Materialism' in Sandra Harding (ed.), *Feminism and Methodology*, Milton Keynes: Open University Press, pp. 157–180, p. 159.
9. Alison R. Webster, 1995, *Found Wanting: Women, Christianity and Sexuality*, London: Cassell, p. 83.
10. Lisa Isherwood, 1996, 'Liberation' in Isherwood and McEwan (eds), *An A to Z of Feminist Theology*, pp. 121–122, p. 121.
11. Adele Reinhartz, 1996, 'From Narrative to History: The Resurrection of Mary and Martha' in Athalya Brenner (ed.), *A Feminist Companion*

to the Hebrew Bible in the New Testament, Sheffield: Sheffield Academic Press, pp. 197–204, p. 207.

12. Kenneth Bailey, 1998, 'Mary, Martha and Jesus: A Continuing Reformation', *Priscilla Papers*, Vol. 12, No. 4, pp. 17–18, p. 17.
13. The use of the double vocative indicates Jesus' words are 'couched in sympathetic terms'. I. Howard Marshall, 1978, *The Gospel of Luke*, Exeter: Paternoster, p. 452.
14. Bailey, 1998, 'Mary, Martha and Jesus: A Continuing Reformation', p. 17.
15. ibid.
16. John 6:35; 4:14. This is not, either directly or implicitly, to infer that Christianity is superior to Judaism on the basis of the respective roles they accord women. Indeed, the point of my argument is how *Christianity* has fostered the subordination of women. Or put another way, looking at this text, to compare Jesus' interaction with women in this passage to the treatment of women by the contemporary church, for which the latter is found wanting. Of course, to do this involves exposition of the text with its original historical and narrative context and, hence, some critique of Jewish society at the time of the New Testament. However, it is my intention in handling this text this way to show that it is patriarchal (and indeed other) social norms, embedded in the various cultures, that Jesus disturbs, and that still need disturbing today.
17. Marcia Y. Riggs, 1996, 'Equality' in Letty M. Russell and J. Shannon Clarkson (eds), *Dictionary of Feminist Theologies*, Mowbray: London, p. 85.
18. Rosemary Radford Ruether, 2002, 'The emergence of Christian feminist theology' in Susan Frank Parsons (ed.), *The Cambridge Companion to Feminist Theology*, Cambridge: Cambridge University Press, pp. 3–22, p. 18.
19. Elisabeth Schüssler Fiorenza, 1996, 'G*d at Work in Our Midst: From a Politics of Identity to a Politics of Struggle', *Feminist Theology*, No. 13, pp. 47–72, p. 62.
20. Judith Plaskow and Carol Christ (eds), 1989, *Weaving the Visions. New Patterns in Feminist Spirituality*, San Francisco: Harper and Row, p. 5.
21. The Stationery Office, 2002, *Northern Ireland Census 2001 Key Statistics*, Norwich: The Stationery Office.
22. This figure is taken from the 2001 Life and Times Survey in which the 1800 respondents were asked, 'Apart from special occasions such as weddings, funerals, baptisms and so on, how often nowadays do you attend services or meetings connected with your religion?' For 47% this was once a week or more, for 9% it was 2 or 3 times a month, and for 6% once a month. At least 48% of each age bracket

(from age 18) attend at least once a month, with at least 31% in each age bracket attending once a week or more. See www.ark.ac.uk/nilt/2001/Background/CHATTEND.html.

23. Valerie Morgan and Grace Fraser, 1994, *The Company We Keep: Women Community and Organisations*, Coleraine: Centre for the Study of Conflict, University of Ulster, p. 2.
24. John Whyte, 1991, *Interpreting Northern Ireland*, Oxford: Clarendon Press, p. 26.
25. Frederick F. Boal, Margaret C. Keane and David N. Livingstone, 1997, *Them and Us? Attitudinal Variation Among Churchgoers in Belfast*, Belfast: Institute of Irish Studies, Queen's University, Belfast, p. 3.
26. Generally, Baptists and Brethren are fundamentalist, as are about one in four of the Church of Ireland, whereas Presbyterians and Methodists are equally divided (Frederick W. Boal and David N. Livingstone, 1986, 'Protestants in Belfast: A View from the Inside', *Contemporary Review*, Vol. 248 No. 1443, pp. 169–75). Some authors use the terms 'fundamentalist' and 'evangelical' interchangeably and others would make a distinction between the two, fundamentalism being the more conservative position. While the term fundamentalism today may be associated with both secular and religious phenomena, I use the term here in the latter category and specifically Christian.
27. John Whyte, 1991, *Interpreting Northern Ireland*, Oxford: Clarendon Press, p. 30. This division in Northern Ireland has frequently been referred to as two communities or community identities. Alternative phrasing would be one community, but two traditions. More recently the language of two communities has been criticised because it is seen to foster division. The term cross-community remains valid as it speaks of including all sections of the society.
28. The interviews were carried out between May 1996 and October 1997. Each interview was tape-recorded then transcribed and the majority (45) were between one and a half and two and a half hours duration.
29. In order to contact a diversity of women, rather than have parish based groups, I identified groups/communities of women which between them accommodated the four characteristics of denomination, age, theological outlook and geographical location. Due to the nature of religious life in Northern Ireland it was unlikely that any one group of women could contain a mix of all four characteristics (for example, the tendency of evangelicals and ecumenics to mix in different circles). I therefore identified various groups in order to ensure a good cross-section of women. I contacted 13 groups, ten of which reached province wide and three a specific area within Northern Ireland. In all I circulated over 800 letters to the sample

groups and received 76 responses (almost a ten per cent response rate), 55 of whom I interviewed.

30. The terminology used to describe this church is a matter of contention. Technically 'Roman' indicates the nature of the ritual followed, the church seeing itself as the Catholic Church that is universal, the one founded by Christ. However the term Roman Catholic has by usage become the 'accepted designation of the one true Church and is recognised officially for legal documents and other purposes' (Robert C. Broderick (ed.), 1987, *The Catholic Encyclopaedia*, Nashville: Thomas Nelson, p. 528). Protestant churches, particularly Anglican, also describe themselves as catholic, that is, universal and therefore many within them would prefer the name Roman Catholic to be used for this church to refute its claim as being the one true church. Grace Davie notes that the 'British are the only people to employ the adjective Roman, thus accentuating the foreignness of Catholicism' (Grace Davie, 1994, *Religion in Britain Since 1945: Believing Without Belonging*, Oxford: Blackwell, p. 92). In Ireland the Roman Catholic/Catholic Church itself uses the term Catholic rather than Roman Catholic and I, therefore, use the term Catholic Church in Ireland.
31. The Stationery Office, *Northern Ireland Census 2001 Key Statistics*.
32. For example, Evangelical Presbyterian Church, Free Presbyterian Church of Ulster, Reformed Presbyterian Church of Ireland, Free Methodist Church.

2: GOD IN WHO'S IMAGE?

1. Elizabeth A. Johnson, 1997, *She Who Is: The Mystery of God in Feminist Theological Discourse*, New York: Crossroad.
2. George B. Caird, 1980, *The Language and Imagery of the Bible*, London: Duckworth, p. 133. As he points out, metaphor and literal here refer to type of language not metaphysical reality (see pp. 131–33).
3. Johanna W. H. van Wijk-Bos, 1995, *Reimagining God: The Case for Scriptural Diversity*, Louisville, Kentucky: John Knox Press, p. 35.
4. Gail Ramshaw, 'The Gender of God' in Loades (ed.), *Feminist Theology: A Reader*, pp. 168–180, p. 169.
5. Johnson, *She Who Is*, pp. 4–5.
6. Dualistic thought has its roots in the philosophy of Plato. His concept of reality as divided 'into the world of ideal forms and the material world of shadows and false impressions led him to an understanding of the human self as possessing two unequal and opposing elements. Human beings possess a soul and a body. The soul is in charge of the unruly body with its manifold desires, but the ultimate goal of exis-

tence is for the enlightened soul to escape the confines of the body and return to the world of ideas.' (Beverley Clack, 1995, 'The Denial of Dualism: Thealogical Reflections on the Sexual and the Spiritual', *Feminist Theology,* No. 10, pp. 102–115, p. 107) Later philosophers developed the understanding of God as being in antithesis to all that is material.

7. Johnson, *She Who Is*, p. 35.
8. Mark 2:17; Luke 14:21–23; 18:16; Mark 9:35; 10:42–45; Matthew 21:1–11; Mark 15:1–32.
9. It is another related question, of course, to consider how relevant the metaphor of kingship is in contemporary society. Interestingly the emphasis in the gospels is not so much on the king as the kingdom of God (see also note 1, chapter 1).
10. Brian Wren, 1989, *What Language Shall I Borrow? God Talk in Worship: A Male Response to Feminist Theology*, London: SCM, p. 124.
11. There is, of course, an inherent contradiction between God as male depicted as caring, nurturing, loving, compassionate, but not identifying caring, nurturing, love and compassion as masculine human characteristics.
12. There is, of course, more to the notion of parenthood than that of authority and care, for example, rootedness of existence, sense of belonging, as well as the concepts involved with the idea of God as mother, some of which are explored further in chapter four. Hence, it is necessary for these aspects of parenthood to be reengaged as well as other non-parental images of God if the image of God as parent is to be reclaimed as a source for imaging God that liberates rather than subordinates.
13. Anne Thurston, 1995, *Because of Her Testimony: The Word in Female Experience*, Dublin: Gill and Macmillan, p. 80.
14. Rosemary Radford Ruether, 1983, *Sexism and God-Talk,* Boston: Beacon Press, p. 64.
15. ibid.
16. Ruether, *Sexism and God-Talk*, p. 65.
17. Sallie McFague, 1983, *Metaphorical Theology: Models of God in Religious Language*, London: SCM, p. 167.
18. Johnson, *She Who Is*, p. 152.
19. John Paul II, 1988, *Mulieries Dignitatem (On the Dignity and Vocation of Women)*, Washington, DC: United States Catholic Conference, note 26, p. 98.
20. Lavinia Byrne, 1994, *Woman at the Altar: The Ordination of Women in the Roman Catholic Church*, London: Mowbray, p. 6.
21. Johnson, *She Who Is*, p. 153.
22. Byrne, *Woman at the Altar*, p. 100.

23. Mary Catherine Hilkert, 1995, 'Key Religious Symbols: Christ and God', *Theological Studies*, Vol. 56, No. 2, pp. 341–52.
24. Johnson, *She Who Is*, pp. 151–2.
25. This identification has been a notable part of theological reflection by women of colour. In this regard Catherine Mary Hilkert (1995, 'Key Religious Symbols: Christ and God', *Theological Studies*, Vol. 56, No. 2, pp. 341–352) cites Jacquelyn Grant's (1989, *White Women's Christ and Black Women's Jesus*, Atlanta: Scholars) argument that black women experience Jesus as divine co-sufferer who empowers them in situations of oppression. She also refers to Asian women's recognition of Jesus as the suffering servant and African women's understanding of Christ as having taken on their condition of weakness, misery, injustice and oppression.
26. In 1984 the English artist Edwina Sandys exhibited in the Cathedral Church of St John, New York, a four foot tall bronze sculpture of a crucified woman. The following controversy saw its removal 11 days later. Since this event the term *Christa* has emerged in some Christian feminism as a christological image, itself a controversial issue (Carter Heyward, 'Christa' in Letty M. Russell and J. Shannon Clarkson (eds), 1996, *Dictionary of Feminist Theologies*, London: Mowbray, pp. 39–40).
27. Ironically, while Margaret Argyle herself comments that she initially had concerns over the depiction of female genitalia rather than the figure of a woman on a cross, the controversy that followed the public use of the *Bosnian Christa* (in an ecumenical service in Manchester Cathedral) focused around the Christa itself and not its setting. This was largely because most critics had not even viewed the work for themselves but were responding to hearing of the presence of the Christa at the service (Julie Clague, 1995, 'Interview with Margaret Argyle' *Feminist Theology*, No. 10, pp. 57–68). A replica of the *Bosnian Christa* that Margaret Argyle made has not been allowed to be displayed publicly in one academic theology department 'since it is seen as an inappropriate depiction of divine suffering' (Lisa Isherwood, 1998, 'Editorial', *Feminist Theology*, No. 19, pp. 5–9, p. 7).
28. Julie Clague, 1995, 'Interview with Margaret Argyle' *Feminist Theology* , No. 10, pp. 57–68, p. 67.
29. Cited in Ruth A. Tucker, and Walter Liefeld, 1987, *Daughters of the Church*, Grand Rapids: Zondervan, p. 94.
30. Cited in Mary Catherine Hilkert, 1995, 'Key Religious Symbols: Christ and God', *Theological Studies*, Vol. 56, No. 2, pp. 341–352, p. 345.
31. Johnson, *She Who Is*, p. 74.
32. This does not necessarily imply that speaking about God is to speak only of human values and ideas. Rather that we are the interpreters

of our understanding of God based on our traditions, experiences, beliefs, religious socialisation and so forth.

33. Caird, *The Language and Imagery of the Bible*, p. 178.
34. McFague, *Metaphorical Theology*, p. 149.
35. Johnson, *She Who Is*, p. 5.
36. McFague, *Metaphorical Theology*, p. 150.
37. Beverley Clack, 1995, 'The Denial of Dualism: Thealogical Reflections on the Sexual and the Spiritual', *Feminist Theology,* No. 10, pp. 102–115, p. 104.
38. Sexual differentiation is not mentioned in previous verses dealing with the creation and propagation of non-human species, but only in regard to humanity being made in the image of God. Phyllis Trible, 1978, *God and the Rhetoric of Sexuality*, London: SCM, p. 19.
39. ibid., p. 21.
40. Clack, 'The Denial of Dualism: Thealogical Reflections on the Sexual and the Spiritual', pp. 105–106.
41. Jann Aldredge Clanton, 1990, *In Whose Image?*, London: SCM. She also demonstrated that men's identification with God as male meant an over exalted picture of themselves leading to harmful and disastrous results for their relationships with women. This was in contrast to men whose language and imagery for God was androgynous or gender transcending who were not only more egalitarian in their relationships, but more open to change and risk as well as more independent and autonomous.
42. Dorothee Sölle, 1995, *Theology For Sceptics*, London: Mowbray, p. 37.
43. Janet Morley, 1990, 'I Desire Her With My Whole Heart' in Loades (ed.), *Feminist Theology: A Reader*, pp. 158–164, p. 163.
44. As noted above, for some women these 'feminine' traits have become adopted by the paternal imagery of God as father. In the context of considering how God the father came to be spoken of as possessing motherly qualities, which she demonstrates includes the language of female reproduction, Daphne Hampson states that because the 'father God arrogates all functions to himself, the need for the female has simply been done away with' (1996, *After Christianity*, London: SCM, p. 181).
45. Ruether, *Sexism and God-Talk*, p. 61.
46. Johnson, *She Who Is*, pp. 54–55.
47. Morley, 'I Desire Her With My Whole Heart' in Loades (ed.), *Feminist Theology: A Reader*, p. 162.
48. ibid.
49. Jann Aldredge Clanton, 1990, *In Whose Image?*, London: SCM, p. 83.
50. Daphne Hampson, 1990, *Theology and Feminism*, Oxford: Blackwell, p. 170.

3: HIS AND HER GOSPELS

1. Mary Stewart van Leeuwen (ed.), 1993, *After Eden: Facing The Challenge of Gender Reconciliation*, Grand Rapids: Eerdmans, p. 390.
2. For further discussion on the reality of these inequalities see chapter 6 of Fran Porter, 2002, *Changing Women, Changing Worlds: Evangelical Women in Church, Community and Politics*, Belfast: Blackstaff.
3. Carol Gilligan, 1995, 'Hearing the Difference: Theorizing Connection', *Hypatia*, Vol. 10, No. 2, pp. 120–127, p. 122.
4. Jean Baker Miller, 1991, *Towards a New Psychology of Women*, 2nd edition, London: Penguin, p. 126.
5. Jane Shaw, 1998, 'Gender and the Act of Synod' in Monica Furlong (ed.), *Act of Synod – Act of Folly?*, London: SCM, pp. 14–26, p. 14.
6. The papal letter (dated 29th June 1995) to the women at the 1995 UN World Conference on Women, held in Beijing, roots this notion in an interpretation of Genesis 2:18, which demonstrates that the 'creation of woman is thus marked from the outset by the principle of help'. While the letter states that help is mutual between men and women, it contradicts this claim by stating that the help referred to in Genesis 'is not referring merely to acting but also to being. Womanhood and manhood are complementary not only from the physical and psychological points of view, but also from the ontological.' (Note 7.)
7. Daphne Hampson, 1996, *After Christianity*, London: SCM, p. 192.
8. Cited in Kari Jo Verhulst, 1995 'Gathering in Power and Hope', *Sojourners*, Sept/Oct 1995 pp. 11–12, p. 12.
9. Daphne Hampson, 1996, 'On Power and Gender' in Adrian Thatcher and Elizabeth Stuart (eds), *Christian Perspectives on Sexuality and Gender*, Leominster: Gracewing, pp. 125–140, p. 129.
10. Note 12, The papal letter to the women at the 1995 UN World Conference on Women, Beijing.
11. Barbara Hilkert Andolsen, 1994, 'Agape in Feminist Ethics' in Lois K. Daly (ed.), *Feminist Theological Ethics: A Reader*, Louisville, Kentucky: John Knox Press, pp. 146–159, p. 152.
12. ibid.
13. Baker Miller, *Towards a New Psychology of Women*, p. 62.
14. Carter Heyward, 1996, 'Is a Self-Respecting Christian Woman an Oxymoron: Reflections on a Feminist Spirituality for Justice' in Thatcher and Stuart (eds), *Christian Perspectives on Sexuality and Gender*, pp. 68–83, p. 78.
15. Elisabeth Porter, 1991, *Women and Moral Identity*, Sydney: Allen and Unwin.
16. Hampson, *After Christianity*, p. 106.
17. Baker Miller, *Towards a New Psychology of Women*, pp. xix–xx. In describing women's care of others as 'active participation' Jean Baker

Miller is challenging the masculine view which does not see women's care of others as activity precisely because it involves others and is not in pursuit of their own goals (p. 54).

18. This is not to suggest that a sense of connection must be associated with weakness. Indeed, to 'outgrow the androcentric discourse of separation and independence, we need to understand that connectivity cannot be equated with femininity or dependency' (Catherine Keller, 1997, 'Seeking and Sucking: On Relation and Essence in Feminist Theology' in Rebecca S. Chopp and Sheila Greeve Davaney (eds), *Horizons in Feminist Theology. Identity, Tradition, and Norms*, Minneapolis: Augsburg Fortress, pp. 54–78, p. 78). Catherine Mowry LaCugna has argued that it is the patriarchal conceptualisation of personhood as self-sufficient, not needing another except out of weakness and only able to relate to another after 'first being what it is in itself and by itself', that produces women's subordination to men (1993, 'God in Communion With Us: The Trinity', in Catherine Mowry LaCugna (ed.), *Freeing Theology: The Essentials of Theology in Feminist Perspective*, New York: HarperCollins, pp. 83–114, p. 91).
19. Nancy Chodorow, 1978, *The Reproduction of Mothering. Psychoanalysis and the Sociology of Gender*, Berkeley and Los Angeles, California: University of California Press, p. 169. She suggested that dual parenting was a way of providing a different environment in which male and female children would develop both autonomy and a capacity to care for others. Her views have been criticised for not taking into account the external structural mechanisms of women's oppression and the changing structure of the family such as woman-headed households.
20. Chodorow, *The Reproduction of Mothering*. Jean Baker Miller argues that what men find difficult to deal with, for example, vulnerability and emotion, they project onto women.
21. Hampson, *After Christianity*, p. 193.
22. Carol Gilligan, 1993, *In A Different Voice: Psychological Theory and Women's Development*, Cambridge, MA: Harvard University Press. Carol Gilligan herself has been clear that her different voice is one of theme rather than gender. In other words, while the different voices were gender related, tending to predominate in men and women respectively, she did not suggest this association was absolute and, indeed, also considered the interplay of the two themes in the development of each sex (p. 2).
23. ibid., p. 35.
24. Hampson, *After Christianity* and 1996, 'On Power and Gender' in Thatcher and Stuart (eds), *Christian Perspectives on Sexuality and Gender*, pp. 125–140, p. 129.

25. Mowry LaCugna, 'God in Communion With Us: The Trinity', in Mowry LaCugna (ed.), *Freeing Theology*, pp. 86–7.
26. Matthew 22:34–40; Mark 12:28–34. In the gospels neighbour includes not only friends or those who share a common identity, but also enemies (Matthew 5:43–47; Luke 10:25–37).
27. Linda Woodhead, 1992, 'Feminism and Christian Ethics' in T. Elwes (ed), *Women's Voices: Essays in Contemporary Feminist Theology*, London: Marshal Pickering, pp. 57–82, 164–167, p. 78.
28. John 13:34–35; Matthew 7:12. The Golden Rule was called this because Emperor Alexander Severus (second century AD) reputedly had it inscribed in gold on his wall.
29. Hampson, *After Christianity*, p. 114.
30. ibid.
31. Robin S. Dillon, 1992, 'Toward a Feminist Conception of Self-Respect', *Hypatia*, Vol. 7, No. 1, pp. 52–69, p. 52.
32. ibid., p. 63.
33. ibid., p. 64.
34. She does not, however, see self-sacrifice in and of itself as 'oppressive or denigrating or incompatible with self-respect. For it is possible to give up pursuing my self-interest, even to give up myself, in a self-respecting manner — knowing what I am worth and so knowing the extent and meaning of my sacrifice.' (ibid., p. 63.) I would agree, arguing that the misapplication of the notion of self-sacrifice as a gendered virtue within Christianity is carried out without the sense of self that *self*-sacrifice literally implies. Indeed, Christ's sacrifice which is held up as the model for Christians, is understood within the New Testament itself and in traditional Christian theology as a *self*-giving (John 10:18), without coercion and out of the free choice of Christ from a position of power (namely equality with God, Philippians 2:6). Such a reading does not support an imposed sacrifice of the self (for women or men) any more than does a reading of gospel events which understands Christ to be the victim of oppression as a result of him challenging the injustices of his day. The real dilemma comes, of course, in working out what is the most responsible thing to do in any given situation. While Barbara Hilkert Andolsen states that given 'a world distorted by evil in which sacrifice of self-interest sometimes seems to be the more responsible course of action', a feminist critique of self-sacrifice means it 'can no longer be considered the self-evident Christian solution to every moral conflict' ('Agape in Feminist Ethics' in Daly (ed.), *Feminist Theological Ethics: A Reader*, p. 156).
35. Dillon, 'Toward a Feminist Conception of Self-Respect', p. 63.
36. ibid.

37. Trudy Govier, 1993, 'Self-Trust, Autonomy, and Self-Esteem', *Hypatia*, Vol. 8, No. 1, pp. 99–120, p. 115.
38. Gilligan, *In A Different Voice*.
39. It is because of the enormity of the demands on women that some have argued that the first step to respecting the self is to give up or withdraw from relationships or institutions that continue to suppress the emerging self. 'Selfishness' is required when the sense of identity is weak (Mary Field Belenky, Blythe McVicker Clinchy, Nancy Rule Goldberger, and Jill Mattuck Tarule, 1986, *Women's Ways of Knowing: The Development of Self, Voice, and Mind*, New York: Basic Books, p. 29). In order to find their own selves women need to detach themselves from institutions and relationships in which they have been subordinate. In other words, in order to develop and find their own voice, their own sense of themselves, they need to withdraw from those circumstances which have in the past drowned out their own voice. Sarah Hoagland has argued that in withdrawing from abusive relationships: 'Far from diminishing my ethical self, I am enhancing it.' (1990, 'Some Concerns About Nel Noddings' *Caring*', *Hypatia*, Vol. 5, No. 1, pp. 109–113, p. 111.) This is an alternative to what one woman described as 'women's way' of not recognising their own needs: 'We just close down, pull down the blinds on our own needs very often and get on with the work, and maybe [it's] the only way of surviving in a situation . . . if your own needs are there and . . . you haven't much hope that they'll ever be met, you just try to forget them.'
40. Mary Stewart van Leeuwen (ed.), *After Eden*, p. 437.
41. Hampson, *After Christianity*, p. 77.
42. Ruether, *Sexism and God-Talk*, p. 112.
43. ibid., p. 111.

4: DEFYING DESTINY AND EMBRACING BIOLOGY

1. M. Midgley and J. Hughes, 1997, 'Are Families Out of Date?' in H. L. Nelson (ed.), *Feminism and Families*, London: Routledge, pp. 55–68, p. 65.
2. Maggie Humm, 1995, *Feminist Theory*, 2nd edition, Hemel Hempstead: Prentice Hall/Harvester Wheatsheaf, p. 159.
3. Seeing the potential and/or actual value of marriage in the lives of women does not mitigate against nor is it designed to conceal the reality that marriage and family are the places of most harm to women and children through violence and abuse. Several of the women interviewed spoke of abuses experienced by themselves and others as both adults and children. Research into domestic violence in Northern Ireland supports the view that 'violence is used by men

to assert their authority in the family and maintain women's subordination' (Joan McKiernan and Monica McWilliams, 1997, 'Women, Religion and Violence in the Family' in Anne Byrne and Madeline Leonard (eds), *Women and Irish Society: A Sociological Reader*, Belfast: Beyond the Pale Publications, pp. 327–341, p. 331.

4. Ann Phoenix and Anne Woollett, 1991, 'Introduction' in A. Phoenix, A. Woollett and E. Lloyd (eds), *Motherhood: Meanings, Practices and Ideologies*, London: Sage, pp. 1–12, p. 7.
5. Ann Oakley, 1976, *Housewife*, London: Penguin.
6. Phoenix and Woollett, 1991, 'Motherhood: Social Construction, Politics and Psychology' in Phoenix, Woollett and Lloyd (eds), *Motherhood*, pp. 13–27, p. 13.
7. Oakley, *Housewife*, p. 199.
8. ibid.
9. Elaine Graham, 1995, *Making The Difference: Gender, Personhood and Theology*, London: Mowbray, p. 226.
10. Adrienne Rich, 1977, *Of Woman Born: Motherhood as Experience and Institution*, London: Virago, p. 13.
11. Infertility being defined as an inability to conceive after an established time period. Infertility may also be experienced by those with a child/children who have had difficulty in conceiving, those who have been unable to have as many children as they would wish, and by those who have fostered/adopted children.
12. Woollett, 1991, 'Having Children: Accounts of Childless Women and Women with Reproductive Problems' in Phoenix, Woollett and Lloyd (eds), *Motherhood*, pp. 47–65.
13. ibid., p. 59.
14. Paula Nicolson, 1997, 'Motherhood and Women's Lives' in Victoria Robinson and Diane Richardson (eds), *Introducing Women's Studies*, 2nd edition, Basingstoke and London: Macmillan Press, pp. 375–399, p. 377.
15. ibid., p. 376.
16. Mary O'Brien cited in Phyllis Kaminski, 1992, '"Reproducing the World": Mary O'Brien's Theory of Reproductive Consciousness and Implications for Feminist Incarnational Theology', *Horizons*, Vol. 19, No. 2, pp. 240–262, p. 242.
17. Paula Nicolson comments that the way post-natal depression has been constructed by medical discourses as an illness has contributed to normalising the idea of child-bearing and early motherhood as unqualified happy (or at least non-depressive) experiences. This not only perpetuates an idealised motherhood but pathologises what is, given the demanding, stressful and at times depressing experience of having a baby, a response that should be expected (see 'Motherhood

and Women's Lives' in Robinson and Richardson (eds), *Introducing Women's Studies*). As Jane Knowles comments from her clinical work with women with young children: 'Of the many women I see in counseling, I am struck by the normality of the psyches and the ridiculous nature of the demands placed upon them. In some ways their "illness" is usually a statement that at some level they too know that what is expected of them is ridiculous but have no ideas or models of how to escape to a more self-defined existence of mothering in ways suitable to themselves.' (1990, 'Woman-Defined Motherhood' in J. P. Knowles and E. Cole (eds), *Motherhood: A Feminist Perspective*, New York and London: The Haworth Press, pp. 1–7, p. 4.)

18. Oakley, *Housewife*, p. 193.
19. See, for example, Alvin Schmidt, 1989, *Veiled and Silenced: How Culture Shaped Sexist Theology*, Macon, Georgia: Mercer University Press.
20. Mary Stewart van Leeuwen notes that making these aspects of women's lives issues of no importance or unacceptable in public conversation is a means of silencing women (see Stewart van Leeuwen (ed.), *After Eden*, pp. 369–374). An example of the practical consequences of this was reported at the 1995 UN World Conference on Women held in Beijing. While women, with their children, comprise nearly 80 per cent of the world's refugees, men make virtually all the decisions about and within refugee camps including the matter of supplies. When Marie Lobo, a senior official with the UN High Commission for Refugees, visited refugee camps in former Yugoslavia she insisted on talking to the women and learned, among other things, that the women had felt unable to tell the males they had spoken to of their need for sanitary towels. She insisted that such be included in the family packs distributed to the camps 'despite the "fuss" her male colleagues made. "Imagine opening up a family pack and finding sanitary towels!" they said. As if it were something horrifying, something outrageous – not something completely normal.' (Kari Jo Verhulst, 1995 'Gathering in Power and Hope', *Sojourners*, Sept/Oct 1995 pp. 11–12, p. 11.) The public acceptance of exposed female breasts for male sexual gratification in posters, pin-ups and tabloid newspapers contrasts with women's experience of breast-feeding in public places for people 'are confused by the public display of a breast in circumstances that are clearly not sexual (Clare Short, 1991, *Dear Clare . . . This is what women feel about page 3*, London: Radius, p. 119).
21. Elaine Graham, 1999, 'Words Made Flesh: Women, Embodiment and Practical Theology', *Feminist Theology*, No. 21, pp. 109–121, p. 115.
22. ibid., p. 111.
23. Sallie McFague, 1987, *Models of God: Theology for an Ecological, Nuclear Age*, London: SCM, p. 116.

24. ibid., p. 113.
25. This is often overlooked. Take, for example, the response of a woman (not an interviewee) to my pointing out that in Luke 15 God is pictured through male (father looking out for his prodigal son and shepherd searching for his lost sheep) and female (woman searching for her lost coin) imagery. For her, my drawing attention to how God was pictured as a woman was to 'bring gender into it' in a way that was not there when God was depicted through male imagery of father or shepherd.
26. This has biblical precedent. As Elizabeth Johnson notes, the 'Jewish and Christian Scriptures recognize the importance of the mother – child relationship when they use the metaphors of pregnancy and birth, suckling and feeding, carrying and training, the anger of the mother bear and the protective wing of the mother hen to refer to God's creative relationship with the world.' (*She Who Is*, p. 171.)
27. Graham, 'Words Made Flesh: Women, Embodiment and Practical Theology', *Feminist Theology*, p. 118.
28. Anne Thurston, 1995, *Because of Her Testimony: The Word in Female Experience*, Dublin: Gill and Macmillan, pp. 100–101.

5: 'SUBORDINATED INSIDERS'

1. Margaret Lamberts Bendroth, 1993, *Fundamentalism and Gender: 1875 to the Present*, New Haven: Yale University Press, p. 75.
2. Four years after the first ordinations of women in the Church of England, a survey conducted among women priests in six Church of England dioceses by the clergy section of the Manufacturing, Science and Finance Union revealed 75 per cent of the interviewees (and therefore over one fifth of the women clergy in these areas) reporting some form of harassment or bullying (the majority from male colleagues but also some from parishioners). Forty per cent had experienced verbal abuse, 37 per cent had experienced exclusion in terms of being isolated or 'cold-shouldered', 23 per cent had been subject to harassment of various types and ten per cent had suffered some form of physical abuse (*Are Anglican Women Priests being Bullied and Harassed? A Survey by MSF Clergy and Church Workers*, February 1998). One senior Synod member, having seen the results of the survey, commented: 'It is way beyond sexism or chauvinism, it is downright misogyny, women priests feeling hated and devalued by their own colleagues.' (Martin Wroe, 'Women Priests Accuse Clergy of Harassment and Bullying', *The Observer Review*, 5 April 1998, p. 1.)
3. For example, the Presbyterian Church in Ireland has ordained

women as elders since the 1920s and yet estimates are that women make up little more than ten per cent of the total.

4. For example, Mark Chaves has argued that in American church institutions ordaining women has taken on the symbolic value of signalling acceptance of the principle of gender equality advocated in the wider society, rather than representing attention to implementing women's equal access. In other words, the possibility of formal access to ordination in a denomination is not the same thing as actualising that experience in full for women. (Mark Chaves, 1999, *Ordaining Women: Culture and Conflict in Religious Organisations*, Cambridge, MA: Harvard University Press.)
5. Lesley Carroll, 1992, 'Panellists: Where Do We Go from Here?' in Phil Kilroy (ed.), *A Conference on 'Women and Religion in Northern Ireland'*, Coleraine: Centre for Research on Women, University of Ulster, pp. 40–42, p. 40.
6. On 15 March 1994 in a letter from the Congregation for Divine Worship and the Discipline of the Sacraments, which clarified the church's position in regard to the laity carrying out liturgical functions, permission was given for girls as well as boys to function as servers at the altar in this role of assisting at the celebration of the Eucharist. The practice of girls as altar servers, however, is entirely at the discretion of each bishop and 'the permission given in this regard by some bishops can in no way be considered as binding on other bishops' (aforementioned letter cited in Catholic briefing paper of 28 April 1994). Further, the decision to allow girls to perform this function is described as a 'decision adopted by certain bishops for specific local reasons' and all the liturgical services such as lectors or ministers of the word (who read the lessons during the mass) and eucharistic ministers (who assist the priest in distributing the Eucharist to the congregation) 'are carried out by lay people . . . according to the judgement of the bishop, without lay people, be they men or women, having any right to exercise them'.
7. For further discussion on the 'token' experience see Fran Porter, 2002, *Changing Women, Changing Worlds: Evangelical Women in Church, Community and Politics*, Belfast: Blackstaff Press and Centre for Contemporary Christianity in Ireland, pp. 69–72.
8. It would not, however, remove the potential conflict between priesthood and caring for a dependent parent, which still tends to fall to women. Nor would it remove the philosophical or theological issues surrounding motherhood and priesthood.
9. Dale Spender, 1990, *Man Made Language*, London: HarperCollins.
10. Veronica Zundel, 1988, 'Women Have a Word For It', *Third Way*, Vol. 11, No. 5, pp. 21–23, p. 21.

11. Monica Furlong, 1991, *A Dangerous Delight: Women and Power in the Church*, London: SPCK.
12. ibid., p. 72.
13. Stewart van Leeuwen (ed.), *After Eden*, p. 344.
14. Janet Finch, 1993, '"It's Great To Have Someone To Talk To": Ethics and Politics of Interviewing Women' in M. Hammersley (ed.), *Social Research: Philosophy, Politics and Practice*, Buckingham: Open University Press, pp. 166–180, p. 175–6.
15. Daphne Hampson (ed.), 1996, *Swallowing A Fishbone?: Feminist Theologians Debate Christianity*, London: SPCK, p. 1.
16. Letty M. Russell, 1993, *Church in the Round: Feminist Interpretation of the Church*, Louisville, Kentucky: Westminster John Knox Press, p. 11.
17. ibid.
18. ibid., p. 12.
19. ibid., p. 27. In order to do this she argues it is necessary to identify where both margin and centre are located in any particular social structure in order to make appropriate responses. We face the choice to align ourselves with either margin or centre or of choosing not to engage with our location, wherever that may be, thereby doing nothing to challenge structures which marginalise.
20. Ruether, *Sexism and God-Talk*, p. 193.
21. ibid., pp. 206–7.
22. ibid., p. 203.
23. Anne Thurston, 1995, *Because of Her Testimony: The Word in Female Experience*, Dublin: Gill and Macmillan, pp. 109–114.
24. Ruether, *Sexism and God-Talk*, p. 205.
25. ibid.
26. Russell, *Church in the Round*.
27. Miriam Therese Winter, Adair Lummis and Allison Stokes, 1994, *Defecting in Place: Women Claiming Responsibility for their own Spiritual Lives*, New York: Crossroad.
28. Ruether, 1994, 'Defecting in Place: Reflections on Women's Spiritual Quest and New Support Groups' in ibid., pp. 248–252, p. 252.

6: THE 'IN-THE-MIDDLE' GOD

1. The term 'the troubles' refers to the conflict in Northern Ireland from 1969 onwards. With the recent phase of the peace process involving the 1998 Belfast Agreement and its aftermath, the term post-troubles is being used. Interviews of those in this book were carried out before this agreement was signed and implemented. Northern Ireland is still a society engaged in a peace process, for while paramilitary ceasefires have led to a significant reduction in sectarian violence, the situation

remains vulnerable. In order to continue rebuilding society, the people of Northern Ireland must find ways, in addition to political settlements, to deal with the many legacies of the past.

2. Part of the definition of sectarianism as defined by Joseph Liechty and Cecelia Clegg (2001, *Moving Beyond Sectarianism*, Dublin, Columba) is that it is a 'system of attitudes, actions, beliefs and structures – at personal, communal, and institutional levels – which always involves religion and typically involves a negative mixing of religion and politics' (p. 102). It is the inclusion of the negative mixing of religion and politics that typically distinguishes sectarianism from other forms of prejudicial behaviour and discriminatory acts.
3. Any change in Northern Ireland's constitutional status is now dependent upon a majority vote of the people of Northern Ireland and no longer rests solely with the decision of MPs at Westminster who are now obliged to follow the democratic will of the people of Northern Ireland. Further, the Republic of Ireland has amended articles two and three of its constitution so that it no longer claims political jurisdiction by right over Northern Ireland.
4. Sexism is used here in its original sense of prejudice or discrimination against women on the basis of their sex, that is, because they are women, rather than in the way it is sometimes applied as prejudice or discrimination against a person (female or male) on the grounds of their sex.
5. The conscious choice to not judge others or to give them the benefit of the doubt in response to harsh or unfair judgements they had themselves received, was a recurring theme among the women interviewed.
6. The Belfast Agreement includes a commitment to pursue equality of opportunity in relation to nine identities: religion and political opinion, gender, race, disability, age, marital status, dependants, and sexual orientation (section 6).
7. The interviewees came from groups chosen because of their explicit Christian identity rather than on any basis that would overtly relate respondents to the troubles. While this means that the lives and thoughts of many Christian women who are directly involved in community issues in Northern Ireland are not included, the range of experience and response among my interviewees indicates how pervasive the community conflict is.
8. The significance of the systemic nature of sectarianism is, according to Joseph Liechty and Cecelia Clegg, that 'a sectarian system can be maintained by people who, individually, do not have a sectarian bone in their bodies' (*Moving Beyond Sectarianism*, p. 9).
9. She returned at a time when the searching she mentions was a rou-

tine feature of everyday life and there was a greater Army presence throughout Northern Ireland than is the current situation.

10. Marie J. Giblin, 1996, 'Empowerment' in Letty M. Russell and J. Shannon Clarkson (eds), *Dictionary of Feminist Theologies*, London: Mowbray, pp. 83–4, p. 83.
11. The Alliance Party of Northern Ireland was founded in 1970 as a cross-community party advocating an alternative to either Unionism or Nationalism. However, due to the context of community conflict in which a resolution requires addressing the national question, the party has struggled to avoid being seen as a liberal unionist party.
12. Only 18 out of 108 (17%) Members elected to the Northern Ireland Assembly in 2003 were women compared with 40% in the Scottish Parliament and 50% in the Welsh Assembly from elections held in the same year. These figures compare to 13%, 37% and 40% respectively in the first elections to these devolved government bodies in 1998. The 2001 local government elections in Northern Ireland returned 19% of women. In 1999 less than 15% of local government councillors were women compared to a figure of 26% for Great Britain. The 2001 general election saw 3 women among the 18 Northern Ireland MPs at Westminister (17%). While this was only one per cent behind the overall Westminster percentage, they were the first women MPs in Northern Ireland for 27 years. All three MEPs from Northern Ireland are male. Statistics taken from: Equal Opportunities Commission for Northern Ireland, *Where Do Women Figure?*; Yvonne Galligan and Rick Wilford, 1999, 'Women's Political Representation in Ireland', in Yvonne Galligan, Eilis Ward and Rick Wilford (eds), *Contesting Politics: Women in Ireland, North and South*, Oxford: Westview Press, p. 130–48; Becky Gill, 2000, *Losing Out Locally: Women and Local Government*, London: Fawcett, p. 5; Education Commission for Northern Ireland.
13. Eilish Rooney, 1997, 'Women in Party Politics and Local Groups: Findings from Belfast' in Anne Byrne and Madelaine Leonard (eds), *Women and Irish Society: A Sociological Reader*, Belfast: Beyond the Pale Publications, pp. 535–51, p. 537.
14. The Northern Ireland Women's Rights Movement (formed in 1975) emerged out of the Civil Rights Movement, which involved mainly nationalists and was working-class. Many nationalist women gained their first experience of political activism in addressing the issues of poverty, unemployment and housing in their communities. Consequently for many unionist women there is an association between feminism and republicanism.
15. For example, the 1970s saw the creation of the Northern Ireland

Women's Aid Federation in response to the major issue of domestic violence.

16. While addressing all the issues inherent in the peace process, it was the presence of the NIWC that ensured that women's rights were stipulated in the 1998 Belfast Agreement (Kate Fearon, 1999, *Women's Work: The Story of the Northern Ireland Women's Coalition*, Belfast: Blackstaff, pp. 106–7).
17. Elisabeth Porter, 2000, 'Participatory Democracy and the Challenge of Dialogue Across Difference' in Carmel Roulston and Celia Davies (eds), 2000, *Gender, Democracy and Inclusion in Northern Ireland*, Basingstoke: Palgrave, pp. 141–63, p. 143.
18. ibid., p. 145.
19. Fearon, *Women's Work*, p. 74.
20. Porter, 'Participatory Democracy and the Challenge of Dialogue Across Difference' in Roulston and Davies (eds), 2000, *Gender, Democracy and Inclusion in Northern Ireland*, p. 143.
21. Rosemary Ridd, 1986, 'Powers of the Powerless' in Rosemary Ridd and Helen Callaway (eds), *Caught Up in Conflict: Women's Responses to Political Strife*, Basingstoke and London: Macmillan Education, pp. 1–24, pp. 2–3. A stark example of this attitude is in the comments of two male politicians to the elected representatives of the NIWC that they should 'stand behind the loyal men of Ulster' and 'that women must start breeding for Ulster' (Monica McWilliams and Avila Kilmurray, 1997 'Athene on the Loose. The Origins of the Northern Ireland Women's Coalition', *Irish Journal of Feminist Studies*, Vol. 2, No. 1, pp. 1–21, p. 19). The idea that politics is not the place for 'proper' women is reflected in the comments of Ian Paisley Jnr when he responded to a question of whether 'women and children first' would still apply in the event of a shipping disaster such as the Titanic with 'I'm a gentleman. Of course I would stand back and see the women and children off. But there's one exception. If the Women's Coalition were on board, it's every man for himself.' (Gail Walker, 1998, 'Gentlemen to the Very Last', *Belfast Telegraph*, 23 January, p. 12.)
22. Monica McWilliams, 1991, 'Women in Northern Ireland: an Overview' in E. Hughes (ed.), *Culture and Politics in Northern Ireland 1960–1990*, Milton Keynes: Open University Press, pp. 81–100, p. 93; Freda Donoghue, Rick Wilford and Robert Miller, 1997, 'Feminist or Womanist? Feminism, the Women's Movement and Age Difference in Northern Ireland', *Irish Journal of Feminist Studies*, Vol. 2, No. 1, pp. 86–105, p 89.
23. The Northern Ireland conflict involves a religious element, which can be neither excluded from the picture nor made the most prominent

component. As Seamus Dunn states, internal conflicts like that in Northern Ireland are 'varied, intricate and multi-dimensional and so are unresponsive to simple dogmatisms' (1995, 'The Conflict as a Set of Problems' in Seamus Dunn (ed.) *Facets of the Conflict in Northern Ireland*, Basingstoke: Macmillan, pp. 3–14, p. 3). Hence, while the Northern Ireland conflict has a religious component, it is not simply a religious problem. The cultural significance of the churches can be seen in that they are still the largest voluntary social institutions in Northern Ireland with a reach far beyond their committed membership and only 'pubs and drinking clubs can claim similar social centrality' (Duncan Morrow, 1996, 'Churches, Society and Conflict in Northern Ireland' in Arthur Aughey and Duncan Morrow (eds) *Northern Ireland Politics*, London and New York: Longman, pp. 190–8, p. 195). Further, the churches have 'to some extent, unwittingly given political and social hostility an institutional shape and an ideological validity' (Morrow, 'Churches, Society and Conflict in Northern Ireland', p. 196). As Joseph Liechty and Cecelia Clegg (*Moving Beyond Sectarianism*) make clear, sectarianism is a problem intrinsic to those within churches not just those outside. My interviewees' comments on the role of their churches in their community endeavours was mixed: some experiencing help and support, others feeling isolated and judged. Clearly, support from a faith community is invaluable in seeking to confront community divisions. As one woman commented 'the sense that . . . you're not the only one . . . [is] very important . . . in terms of not giving up hope'. Another woman in an inter-church marriage (the term used for marriage between a Catholic and a Protestant) spoke of a community of both Catholics and Protestants with which they were involved as 'the only place that both of us can go to where neither of us feel that we're giving something up for being different or not being accepted'.

24. I use the term prophetic here in the sense of speaking and acting in ways that reveal the realities of a situation that others refuse or are unable to acknowledge.
25. This would also be consistent with the biblical portrayal of God as concerned with justice and liberation. This imagery has been used by some in a triumphalistic fashion to endorse aggressive actions. While such an application of the idea of God as just is not inevitable, the significance of the incarnational model is its emphasis on God sharing in the trauma of human existence and as such experiencing powerlessness rather than exercising transcendent power. It is in the immanence of God in human situations that people are enabled to become empowered, that is, assume responsibility for themselves, rather than impose power over others. While some feminists

criticise the model of the suffering Christ in crucifixion in that it has been used to exemplify a sacrificial model particularly for women, the strength of such a notion, as mentioned in chapter two, is in the identification of God in human vulnerability, which in itself is empowering. To use a concept from feminist theory as introduced in chapter one, in the gospels, the incarnation of Christ is the means whereby God assumes the standpoint of the powerless and hence, experiences the oppression of the people.

ACKNOWLEDGEMENTS

I wish to express my sincere thanks and appreciation, first of all, to the women whose voices and stories appear in this book. Their warmth and welcome made the interview process an immensely enjoyable experience. Without their generous and honest giving of themselves it would not be possible for this book to be as expressive or vivid of the reality of Christian women. Their lives and depth of reflection have continued to energise me in completing this work. My hope is that any of them who might read this book will find it, in the words of one woman speaking of being interviewed, an 'empowering experience . . . It's not only being heard by another person but hearing yourself . . . It's in hearing myself, being heard, and then gaining understanding.'

Of the many people who have contributed to my life over the duration of this project I would like to acknowledge two in particular. Lis Porter, who supervised the original research for my doctoral thesis, provided then and since not only invaluable guidance, encouragement and support but also friendship. Her openness and vitality is refreshing to encounter. Another friend, Liz Campbell, has through her companionship given me that extraordinary gift of sharing vulnerability (along with seasonal supplies of novelty chocolates!) May there be many more monthly brunches!

It was my pleasure to work with DLT in bringing this book

to completion, who have so ably and enthusiastically provided it a home. Particular thanks go to Brendan Walsh, Virginia Hearn and Rachel Davis. I am indebted also to Caroline Hamilton for providing the index.

Finally, to David, whose own engagement in the struggle against human diminishment I so admire, my thanks and love for always choosing the window seat!

INDEX